TEACHER'S PET PUBLICATIONS

LITPLAN TEACHER PACK
for
The Hobbit
based on the book by
J. R. R. Tolkien

Written by
Mary B. Collins

© 2001 Teacher's Pet Publications
All Rights Reserved

This **Lit Plan** for J. R. R. Tolkien's
The Hobbit
has been brought to you by Teacher's Pet Publications, Inc.

Copyright Teacher's Pet Publications 2001
11504 Hammock Point
Berlin MD 21811

Only the student materials in this unit plan
such as worksheets, study questions, assignment sheets, and tests
may be reproduced multiple times for use in the purchaser's classroom.

For any additional copyright questions,
contact Teacher's Pet Publications.

www.tpet.com

PUBLISHER'S NOTE
Several pages in this LitPlan have been left blank to facilitate two-sided printing.

TABLE OF CONTENTS - *The Hobbit*

Introduction	5
Unit Objectives	7
Reading Assignment Sheet	8
Unit Outline	9
Study Questions (Short Answer)	13
Quiz/Study Questions (Multiple Choice)	34
Pre-reading Vocabulary Worksheets	69
Lesson One (Introductory Lesson)	85
Nonfiction Assignment Sheet	89
Oral Reading Evaluation Form	90
Writing Assignment 1	86
Writing Assignment 2	93
Writing Assignment 3	100
Writing Evaluation Form	96
Vocabulary Review Activities	105
Extra Writing Assignments/Discussion ?s	107
Unit Review Activities	110
Unit Tests	113
Unit Resource Materials	149
Vocabulary Resource Materials	177

A FEW NOTES ABOUT THE AUTHOR
J. R. R. Tolkien

J. R. R. (John Ronald Ruel) Tolkien was born January 3, 1892 in South Africa, where his father worked as a bank manager. Both of his parents were from Birmingham, England, which is where he returned in 1896.

He was orphaned at the age of 14 and was left in the care of a Roman Catholic priest. He served in World War I and later became a professor at Oxford University. He married Edith Mary Bratt in 1916 and had four children. Tolkien died on September 2, 1973.

J. R. R. Tolkien's major works include *The Hobbit* (1937), *The Fellowship of the Ring* (1954), *The Two Towers* (1955) and *The Return of the King* (1956).

INTRODUCTION

This unit has been designed to develop students' reading, writing, thinking, and language skills through exercises and activities related to *The Hobbit* by J. R. R. Tolkien. It includes twenty lessons, supported by extra resource materials.

The **introductory lesson** introduces students to the idea of an adventure through a writing assignment. Following the introductory activity, students are given an explanation of how the activity relates to the book they are about to read.

The **reading assignments** are approximately thirty pages each; some are a little shorter while others are a little longer. Students have approximately 15 minutes of pre-reading work to do prior to each reading assignment. This pre-reading work involves reviewing the study questions for the assignment and doing some vocabulary work for some vocabulary words they will encounter in their reading.

The **study guide questions** are fact-based questions; students can find the answers to these questions right in the text. These questions come in two formats: short answer or multiple choice The best use of these materials is probably to use the short answer version of the questions as study guides for students (since answers will be more complete), and to use the multiple choice version for occasional quizzes. If your school has the appropriate machinery, it might be a good idea to make transparencies of your answer keys for the overhead projector.

The **vocabulary work** is intended to enrich students' vocabularies as well as to aid in the students' understanding of the book. Prior to each reading assignment, students will complete a two-part worksheet for several vocabulary words in the upcoming reading assignment. Part I focuses on students' use of general knowledge and contextual clues by giving the sentence in which the word appears in the text. Students are then to write down what they think the words mean based on the words' usage. Part II nails down the definitions of the words by giving students dictionary definitions of the words and having students match the words to the correct definitions based on the words' contextual usage. Students should then have an understanding of the words when they meet them in the text.

After each reading assignment, students will go back and formulate answers for the study guide questions. Discussion of these questions serves as a **review** of the most important events and ideas presented in the reading assignments.

There is a **vocabulary review** lesson which pulls together all of the fragmented vocabulary lists for the reading assignments and gives students a review of all of the words they have studied.

Following the reading of the book, a lesson is devoted to the **extra discussion questions/writing assignments**. These questions focus on interpretation, critical analysis and personal response, employing a variety of thinking skills and adding to the students' understanding of the novel. The discussion question list has been shortened in this unit because of the **project** that is included. It takes many of the topics that would normally be discussed in the extra discussion questions lesson and has students focus on those items in greater detail. Two lessons are devoted to individual or group reports about these topics.

There are three **writing assignments** in this unit, each with the purpose of informing, persuading, or having students express personal opinions. The first assignment is to write about an adventure they have had or would like to have. It gives students the opportunity to express their own thoughts and ideas, and to practice some creative writing. The second assignment gives students the opportunity to practice writing persuasively. They are to persuade Bilbo either to go or not to go with Thorin & Co. The third assignment is to give students a chance to write an informative composition. It serves the dual purpose of helping students focus and organize the information they have gathered while working on their projects and helping the teacher evaluate the project work.

In addition, there is a **nonfiction reading assignment**. Students are required to read a piece of nonfiction related in some way to *The Hobbit*. After reading their nonfiction pieces, students will fill out a worksheet on which they answer questions regarding facts, interpretation, criticism, and personal opinions. During one class period, students make **oral presentations** about the nonfiction pieces they have read. This not only exposes all students to a wealth of information, it also gives students the opportunity to practice **public speaking**.

The **review lesson** pulls together all of the aspects of the unit. The teacher is given four or five choices of activities or games to use which all serve the same basic function of reviewing all of the information presented in the unit.

The **unit test** comes in two formats: multiple choice-matching-true/false or short answer. As a convenience, two different tests for each format have been included. There is also an advanced short answer unit test that is more difficult than the other tests.

There are additional **support materials** included with this unit. The **unit and vocabulary resource sections** include suggestions for an in-class library, crossword and word search puzzles related to the novel, and extra worksheets. There is a list of **bulletin board ideas** which gives the teacher suggestions for bulletin boards to go along with this unit. In addition, there is a list of **extra class activities** the teacher could choose from to enhance the unit or as a substitution for an exercise the teacher might feel is inappropriate for his/her class. **Answer keys** are located directly after the **reproducible student materials** throughout the unit. The student materials may be reproduced for use in the teacher's classroom without infringement of copyrights. No other portion of this unit may be reproduced without the written consent of Teacher's Pet Publications, Inc.

UNIT OBJECTIVES - *The Hobbit*

1. Through reading Tolkien's *The Hobbit*, students will gain a better understanding of the of good versus evil, appearances versus reality, bravery versus cowardice, and other themes in the book

2. Students will demonstrate their understanding of the text on four levels: factual, interpretive, critical and personal.

3. Students will examine Bilbo's character development.

4. Students will each study a particular aspect of the book and prepare oral and written reports.

5. Students will describe an adventure they have had or would like to have.

6. Students will be given the opportunity to practice reading aloud and silently to improve their skills in each area.

7. Students will answer questions to demonstrate their knowledge and understanding of the main events and characters in *The Hobbit* as they relate to the author's theme development.

8. Students will enrich their vocabularies and improve their understanding of the novel through the vocabulary lessons prepared for use in conjunction with the novel.

9. The writing assignments in this unit are geared to several purposes:
    a. To have students demonstrate their abilities to inform, to persuade, or to express their own personal ideas
    >Note: Students will demonstrate ability to write effectively to <u>inform</u> by developing and organizing facts to convey information. Students will demonstrate the ability to write effectively to <u>persuade</u> by selecting and organizing relevant information, establishing an argumentative purpose, and by designing an appropriate strategy for an identified audience. Students will demonstrate the ability to write effectively to <u>express personal ideas</u> by selecting a form and its appropriate elements.
    b. To check the students' reading comprehension
    c. To make students think about the ideas presented by the novel
    d. To encourage logical thinking
    e. To provide an opportunity to practice good grammar and improve students' use of the English language.

READING ASSIGNMENT SHEET - *The Hobbit*

Date Assigned	Reading Assignment	Completion Date
	Chapter 1	
	Chapters 2-3	
	Chapters 4-5	
	Chapter 6	
	Chapter 7	
	Chapter 8	
	Chapters 9-10	
	Chapters 11-12	
	Chapters 13-15	
	Chapters 16-19	

UNIT OUTLINE - *The Hobbit*

1 Introduction Writing Assignment 1	2 Materials PVR 1	3 Study ?s 1 PVR 2-3	4 Writing Assignment 2 PV 4-5	5 Study ?s 2-3 Read 4-5
6 Study ?s 4-5 PVR 6	7 Study ?s 6 PVR 7 Writing Conf.	8 Study ?s 7 Project PVR 8	9 Project	10 Study ?s 8 PVR 9-10
11 Study ?s 9-10 Project PVR 11-12	12 Study ?s 11-12 Library Nonfiction Asst. PVR 13-15	13 Study ?s 13-15 Nonfiction Discussion PVR 16-19	14 Study ?s 16-19 Writing Assignment 3	15 Vocab Review
16 Extra Discussion ?s	17 Project Presentations	18 Project Presentations	19 Unit Review	20 Unit Test

Key: P = Preview Study Questions   V = Vocabulary Work   R = Read

STUDY GUIDE QUESTIONS

SHORT ANSWER STUDY GUIDE QUESTIONS - *The Hobbit*

Chapter 1

1. List 10 characteristics of hobbits.
2. Identify (leave room to make additional notes about these characters as you read the book):
    Bilbo Baggins
    Belladonna Took
    Bingo Baggins
    Gandalf
    Dwalin
    Balin
    Kili & Fili
    Dori
    Nori
    Ori
    Oin
    Gloin
    Bifur
    Bofur
    Bombur
    Thorin

3. What was unusual about the Tooks?
4. Why did Gandalf visit Bilbo Baggins?
5. Who was Bilbo expecting for tea?
6. What about his uninvited guests irked Bilbo?
7. What effect did the dwarves' singing have on Bilbo?
8. State Gloin's opinion of Bilbo Baggins.
9. Gandalf showed the dwarves something that belonged to Thorin's grandfather. What was it?
10. Identify Dale.
11. Identify Smaug.
12. What story did Thorin tell Bilbo?
13. How did Gandalf get the map and key?
14. Identify Azog the Goblin.

Chapter 2

1. Why did Bilbo leave his Hill in such a hurry to go to the Green Dragon Inn?
2. What had Bilbo forgotten to bring with him, and how was it remedied?
3. When did Bilbo first wish that he were back home?
4. Identify William, Bert, and Tom.

Hobbit Short Answer Study Questions Page 2

    5. What did William catch Bilbo doing?
    6. Who saved Bilbo, Thorin, and company from the trolls? How?
    7. What did Gandalf, Thorin, and Bilbo take from the trolls' cave?

Chapter 3
1. What kind of creatures inhabited the valley of Rivendell and helped the travelers find the Last Homely Home? What did Bilbo and the dwarves think of them?
2. Identify Elrond.
3. What important information did Elrond give the travelers?
4. What was Durin's Day?

Chapter 4
1. Why did the travelers go into the cave?
2. What did Bilbo dream in the cave?
3. Bilbo and Thorin & Co. had a nasty surprise in the cave. What was it?
4. Did the goblins get Gandalf?
5. List several characteristics of goblins.
6. What caused the Great Goblin to become enraged?
7. How did the travelers escape from the Goblins' cavern?
8. What were Biter and Beater?
9. Goblins run faster than dwarves. How did the travelers escape the pursuit of the goblins?
10. What happened to Dori and Bilbo?

Chapter 5
1. When Bilbo awoke after falling off of Dori's shoulders when the goblins grabbed Dori, what was strange about his surroundings?
2. While groping around on the floor, what did Bilbo find and put in his pocket?
3. How did Bilbo know his knife was an elvish blade, too?
4. Identify Gollum.
5. Gollum and Bilbo made a deal. What was it?
6. How did Bilbo win the riddle game with Gollum?
7. Where was Gollum's lost birthday present?
8. How did Bilbo discover the power of the ring?
9. How did Bilbo find the way out of Gollum's land?
10. Why didn't Bilbo kill Gollum?
11. What gave Bilbo away to the goblins as he tried to escape out the door?
12. Why did the goblins give up looking for Bilbo?

Hobbit Short Answer Study Questions Page 3

Chapter 6
1. Why did the dwarves have a better opinion of Bilbo Baggins when he rejoined them after his adventures with Gollum and the goblins?
2. What detail about his adventures with Gollum did Bilbo leave out when he told the dwarves the story?
3. Where were the travelers after the goblin adventures?
4. Why did the travelers climb up into the trees?
5. Who saved Bilbo from the wolves?
6. Identify wargs.
7. Why were the wargs at the clearing?
8. How did Gandalf try to get rid of the wargs and goblins?
9. Who or what saved the travelers from the wargs, goblins, and fire?
10. Describe the Eagles.

Chapter 7
1. Identify Beorn.
2. Why did Gandalf introduce the dwarves a few at a time to Beorn?
3. What news did Gandalf bring the dwarves about Beorn's whereabouts?
4. Beorn warned them about some things in Mirkwood. What?
5. How do we know Beorn liked the travelers?
6. Why did Gandalf leave Thorin & Co.?
7. What were Gandalf's parting words to the travelers as he left them at Mirkwood?

Chapter 8
1. Describe Mirkwood.
2. How did the travelers cross the black water?
3. What happened to Bombur at the black river crossing?
4. What did Bilbo see from the top of the oak tree in Mirkwood?
5. Why did the travelers leave the path?
6. What happened when they entered the ring of light to beg for food?
7. How did Bilbo get separated from the others in Mirkwood?
8. What made Bilbo feel fierce and bold?
9. Identify Sting.
10. How did Bilbo rescue the dwarves from the spiders?
11. Who was missing after the travelers were rescued from the spiders?
12. How did Thorin get separated from the others?

Hobbit Short Answer Study Questions Page 4

Chapter 9
1. Why were the travelers actually glad to be captured by the wood elves?
2. How did Bilbo keep from getting captured by the wood elves?
3. How did Bilbo rescue Thorin & Co. from the Elvenking?

Chapter 10
1. What sight did Bilbo see as he floated along on the barrel-raft?
2. How had Bilbo and the travelers been lucky?
3. What songs did men near Long Lake still sing?
4. Why did Thorin demand to be taken to the Master of the Men of the Lake?
5. Why did the Master treat the travelers well, and send them to the mountain with provisions?

Chapter 11
1. Why did the men of the town leave the travelers at the end of the third day?
2. Identify Ravenhill.
3. What did the scouting party see at the front gate?
4. What were the dwarves looking for on the western side of the mountain?
5. How did the dwarves get the secret door open?

Chapter 12
1. What did Bilbo see at the end of the tunnel?
2. Why did Smaug go into a rage upon awakening?
3. Why did Bilbo go back down the tunnel a second time?
4. How did Bilbo answer when the dragon asked who he was?
5. Which of Smaug's senses was very keen?
6. What was Smaug's weakness that Bilbo discovered?
7. Why did Thorin tell Bilbo to leave the thrush alone?
8. Why did the dwarves move their camp to within the tunnel?
9. What did Thorin say was the greatest treasure of the Mountain?

Chapter 13
1. Why did Thorin & Co. go down the tunnel?
2. What did Bilbo put in his deepest pocket?
3. How did Thorin & Co. get out of the Mountain?
4. Where did the travelers go after they got out of the Mountain?
5. Identify "cram."

Hobbit Short Answer Study Questions Page 5

Chapter 14
1. Identify Esgaroth.
2. Identify Bard.
3. How did Bard know where to aim when he shot Smaug?
4. What was Bard's reward for killing the dragon?
5. What was Bard's response to the Master's offer?
6. Who came to help the Lake people, at Bard's request?
7. Why did all the men of arms go to the Mountain?

Chapter 15
1. Identify Roäc.
2. What did Thorin ask Roäc to do?
3. What did Bard ask of Thorin, and what was Thorin's response?
4. What did the messenger from Esgaroth declare?

Chapter 16
1. What news did Roäc bring the besieged dwarves?
2. Why did Bilbo offer to take Bombur's watch?
3. What did Bilbo give Bard? Why?
4. Who praised Bilbo for his meeting with Bard?

Chapter 17
1. Why did Thorin throw Bilbo out of his camp?
2. Why wouldn't Bard let Dain and the dwarves pass?
3. What announcement did Gandalf make?
4. What were the armies in The Battle of Five Armies?
5. What plan did Gandalf propose?
6. Why did the dwarves agree to fight with the men and elves against the goblins and wargs?
7. Who were the first to charge against the goblins?
8. When all seemed lost against the goblins, what appeared on the scene?
9. What happened to Bilbo during the battle?

Chapter 18
1. When Bilbo awoke after being knocked out by the stone, what did he see?
2. Why did Thorin call for Bilbo?
3. What did Bilbo miss at the end of the battle while he was knocked out?
4. What parting gift did Bard bestow upon Thorin?
5. What parting gift did the Elvenking give Thorin?
6. Who led the dwarves after Thorin's death?

Hobbit Short Answer Study Questions Page 6

7. What did Dain give Bard? Why?
8. What did Bard do with his riches?
9. What did Bilbo give the Elvenking? Why?
10. Who became a great chief, ruling lands between the mountains and the wood?

Chapter 19
1. Where had Gandalf been while he was away from Thorin and Co.?
2. What did Gandalf and Bilbo dig up?
3. When Bilbo arrived home, what did he find?
4. What, besides spoons, did Bilbo lose?
5. Who came to visit Bilbo a few years after his return home?
6. What news did Balin bring?
7. What were Gandalf's last words to Bilbo in this book?

ANSWER KEY: SHORT ANSWER STUDY GUIDE QUESTIONS - *The Hobbit*

Chapter 1

1. List 10 characteristics of hobbits.
    half our height, no beards, no magic, fat stomachs, dress in bright colors, feet have leathery soles and hairy tops, good natured faces, long brown fingers, plain & quiet folk, no use for adventure, love to eat smoke & blow smoke rings, used to tunneling, do not lose sense of direction underground, move quietly, hide easily, recover from falls and bruises, have wisdom and wise sayings, love to eat frequently

2. Identify (leave room to make additional notes about these characters as you read the book):
    Bilbo Baggins   The story is about Bilbo Baggins, a hobbit, and his adventures as he helps some dwarves get to Lonely Mountain to regain their kingdom.
    Belladonna Took was Bilbo's mother. She was the daughter of Old Took.
    Bingo Baggins was Bilbo's father.
    Gandalf is a wizard. He wears a tall, pointed, blue hat and immense black boots, and he has a long beard and bushy eyebrows. He chooses Bilbo to go with the dwarves.
    Dwalin - dwarf, blue beard, golden belt, bright eyes, dark green hood, plays violin, Balin's brother
    Balin - dwarf, old looking, white beard, scarlet hood, plays violin, Dwalin's brother
    Kili & Fili - dwarves, blue hoods, silver belts, yellow beards, bag of tools and a spade, played fiddles, sharp vision
    Dori - dwarf, purple hood, played flute, carried Bilbo a lot
    Nori - dwarf, purple hood, played flute
    Ori - dwarf, gray hood, played flute
    Oin - dwarf, brown hood
    Gloin - dwarf, white hood
    Bifur - dwarf, yellow hood, played clarinet
    Bofur - dwarf, yellow hood, played clarinet
    Bombur - dwarf, pale green hood, fat & heavy, played drum
    Thorin - dwarf, sky blue hood, long silver tassel, last name Oakenshield, golden harp, The trip is to regain his family's kingdom from Smaug, the dragon.

3. What was unusual about the Tooks?
    There was something un-hobbit like about them; they were adventurous.

4. Why did Gandalf visit Bilbo Baggins?
    Gandalf came to tell Bilbo about an adventure he had planned.

5. Who was Bilbo expecting for tea?
    Bilbo was expecting Gandalf.

6. What about his uninvited guests irked Bilbo?
    They came right in and made themselves at home, placing orders for food and drink.

7. What effect did the dwarves' singing have on Bilbo?
    It awoke the Took in him, his adventurous spirit.

8. State Gloin's opinion of Bilbo Baggins.
    He thinks Gandalf has made a mistake, that Bilbo is a coward, not a brave burglar.

9. Gandalf showed the dwarves something that belonged to Thorin's grandfather. What was it?
    It was a map of the Mountain, showing a secret entrance. He also had a key.

10. Identify Dale.
    Dale was a dwarf-town in ruins in the shadow of the mountain.

11. Identify Smaug.
    Smaug was the name of the dragon that overtook the dwarves' mountain kingdom, the surrounding area, and the riches therein.

12. What story did Thorin tell Bilbo?
    He explained that his grandfather was King of the Mountain and had vast riches. The dragon Smaug came from the North, destroyed his kingdom, killed the dwarves, took the treasure, and moved into the mountain.

13. How did Gandalf get the map and key?
    Before he left, Thorin's father gave it to him to give to Thorin.

14. Identify Azog the Goblin.
    He killed Thorin's grandfather, Thror.

Chapter 2
1. Why did Bilbo leave his Hill in such a hurry to go to the Green Dragon Inn?
    He was late to meet Thorin and Company to begin the adventure.

2. What had Bilbo forgotten to bring with him, and how was it remedied?
    He forgot his hat, walking stick, money, handkerchief, provisions, and clothing. He came with only himself and the clothes on his back. Dwalin gave him a dark green cloak and hood. The dwarves had provisions. Later we learn that Gandalf brings a few things for Bilbo, including his pipe and tobacco.

3. When did Bilbo first wish that he were back home?
    The travelers had passed through the hobbit lands and had gone into the Lone-lands where roads were bad, castles had an evil look, and the weather had turned cold and wet. He was tired and cold and wet.

4. Identify William, Bert, and Tom.
    They were the trolls Bilbo found when he got to the red firelight.

5. What did William catch Bilbo doing?
    Bilbo was trying to pick William's pocket.

6. Who saved Bilbo, Thorin, and company from the trolls? How?
    Gandalf mimicked their voices and got them arguing with each other long enough for the sun to come out and turn them to stone.

7. What did Gandalf, Thorin, and Bilbo take from the trolls' cave?
    Gandalf and Thorin each took swords with jeweled hilts. Bilbo took a knife in a leather sheath.

Chapter 3

1. What kind of creatures inhabited the valley of Rivendell and helped the travelers find the Last Homely Home? What did Bilbo and the dwarves think of them?
    The creatures were elves. Bilbo liked them but was a little frightened of them.
    The Dwarves didn't get on well with them they thought the elves were foolish.

2. Identify Elrond.
    Elrond was the Elvenking who ruled the valley of Rivendell and lived in the Last Homely Home.

3. What important information did Elrond give the travelers?
    1) He identified the swords Gandalf and Thorin had taken from the trolls' cave as being very old swords made by the High Elves of the West, his kin, for the Goblin-wars. Thorin's sword was named Orcrist, the Goblin-cleaver. Gandalf's was named Glamdring, the Foe-hammer, and was once worn by the King of Gondolin.

    2) Elrond read the moon-letters to reveal the way to open the secret door on the side of the mountain.

4. What was Durin's Day?
    It was the first day of the New Year for dwarves.

Chapter 4

1. Why did the travelers go into the cave?
    They wanted shelter from the storm.

2. What did Bilbo dream in the cave?
    He dreamed that the crack in the wall got bigger and bigger and the floor of the cave gave way.

3. Bilbo and Thorin & Co. had a nasty surprise in the cave. What was it?
    Goblins grabbed them and took them underground into their cavern.

4. Did the goblins get Gandalf?
    No.

5. List several characteristics of goblins.
    cruel, wicked, bad-hearted, make no beautiful things (but clever ones & instruments of torture), keep prisoners and slaves, hate everyone and everything (particularly orderly & prosperous), special grudge against Thorin's people because of the Goblin-wars.

6. What caused the Great Goblin to become enraged?
    One of the goblins showed the Great Goblin the sword Thorin carried–Orcrist.

7. How did the travelers escape from the Goblins' cavern?
    Gandalf rescued by making the fire blow up in smoke & sparks, which burned the goblins and caused great confusion. The Great Goblin was slain by Gandalf and the travelers fled in the confusion.

8. What were Biter and Beater?
    They were the goblin names for Orcrist and Glamdring, the swords.

9. Goblins run faster than dwarves. How did the travelers escape the pursuit of the goblins?
    Gandalf and Thorin turned and used Orcrist and Glamdring against them. They killed some goblins and the rest ran in fear of Beater and Biter.

10. What happened to Dori and Bilbo?

    Sneaky goblins came up behind them and grabbed Dori. Bilbo fell from Dori's shoulders, hit his head on a stone, and became unconscious.

Chapter 5

1. When Bilbo awoke after falling off of Dori's shoulders when the goblins grabbed Dori, what was strange about his surroundings?

    He was in total darkness.

2. While groping around on the floor, what did Bilbo find and put in his pocket?

    A ring.

3. How did Bilbo know his knife was an elvish blade, too?

    It glowed, showing goblins were near–but not too near.

4. Identify Gollum.

    He was a small, slimy creature, dark as darkness (except for his two big, round, pale eyes), had large feet, and long fingers. He was quick and quiet. he hissed as he spoke, called himself "precious," and liked riddles. He lost the ring that Bilbo found.

5. Gollum and Bilbo made a deal. What was it?

    They would ask each other riddles. The first to be stumped would lose. If Bilbo won, Gollum would show him the way out. If Gollum won, he would eat Bilbo.

6. How did Bilbo win the riddle game with Gollum?

    He had some good luck, pretended to be bolder than he felt, and the final question he asked wasn't really a riddle, but he got away with it. Gollum didn't know what was in Bilbo's pockets.

7. Where was Gollum's lost birthday present?

    It was in Bilbo's pocket.

8. How did Bilbo discover the power of the ring?

    Gollum suspected Bilbo may have his ring, so he kept asking what Bilbo had in his pockets. That made Bilbo more curious about what he had. Gollum got angrier and came after Bilbo, who slipped the ring on his finger while feeling it in his pocket. Bilbo tripped trying to escape from Gollum, and Gollum went right by him, as if he were not there. Gollum talked to himself aloud, saying he was afraid the goblins would get Bilbo and the ring and use it to become invisible and get *him*.

9. How did Bilbo find the way out of Gollum's land?
   Gollum thought Bilbo already knew the way out, so he hurried to catch him. Bilbo, wearing the ring, followed Gollum to the exit and jumped right over him to escape.

10. Why didn't Bilbo kill Gollum?
    He felt sorry for him.

11. What gave Bilbo away to the goblins as he tried to escape out the door?
    They saw his shadow.

12. Why did the goblins give up looking for Bilbo?
    Goblins don't like the sun; it makes their legs wobble and their heads giddy, so they went back where they had come from rather than stay in the sunlight.

<u>Chapter 6</u>
1. Why did the dwarves have a better opinion of Bilbo Baggins when he rejoined them after his adventures with Gollum and the goblins?
   First, he managed to sneak by Balin, their best watch guard. Then Bilbo told them how he had escaped from Gollum and the goblins. After hearing his story, they thought he was clever, brave, and a good burglar after all.

2. What detail about his adventures with Gollum did Bilbo leave out when he told the dwarves the story?
   He didn't tell them about the ring.

3. Where were the travelers after the goblin adventures?
   They were through the Misty Mountain, on the edge of the Land Beyond.

4. Why did the travelers climb up into the trees?
   They climbed up into the trees to escape the wolves.

5. Who saved Bilbo from the wolves?
   Dori saved him.

6. Identify wargs.
   That's what the evil wolves over the Edge of the Wild were named.

7. Why were the wargs at the clearing?
   They were supposed to conspire with goblins there, but the goblins were late.

8. How did Gandalf try to get rid of the wargs and goblins?
    He lit pine cones on fire with his wand and threw them at the wargs. It worked to cause confusion and to get rid of some of the wolves, but it also set the woods on fire.

9. Who or what saved the travelers from the wargs, goblins, and fire?
    Eagles did. They picked them up and flew them to safety.

10. Describe the Eagles.
    Some eagles were not kindly but were cowardly and cruel. The eagles that rescued the travelers, however, were from the North, and they were proud, strong, and noble-hearted. The goblins hated and feared them.

Chapter 7
1. Identify Beorn.
    Beorn was the Bear-Man who was hospitable to the weary travelers. he gave them food and drink, a place to rest, and provisions for the next part of their journey. He was kind and gentle but could also be fierce. He cared for animals and ate no meat.

2. Why did Gandalf introduce the dwarves a few at a time to Beorn?
    He knew Beorn would never accept so many visitors all at once. By telling their story, he gained Beorn's interest and respect, and by introducing the dwarves a few at a time throughout the story, he gained Beorn's acceptance of the whole group.

3. What news did Gandalf bring the dwarves about Beorn's whereabouts?
    He told them Beorn had been out checking out their story. Gandalf had followed the bear tracks to the Warg clearing.

4. Beorn warned them about some things in Mirkwood. What?
    Beorn warned them about a black stream that crosses the path. He said it causes enchantment, a great drowsiness, and forgetfulness. He also warned them not to leave the path.

5. How do we know Beorn liked the travelers?
    He gave them food and lodging, let them borrow his ponies, and lurked around them watching out for them on their way.

6. Why did Gandalf leave Thorin & Co.?
    He had pressing business in the South.

7. What were Gandalf's parting words to the travelers as he left them at the edge of Mirkwood?
   He told them not to leave the path for any reason.

Chapter 8

1. Describe Mirkwood.
   dark, tangled boughs and matted twigs, queer noises, dark and thick cobwebs, still and stuffy, yellow and green eyes shine at night, bats

2. How did the travelers cross the black water?
   They attached a hook to a rope and threw it to a boat they saw on the other side, to retrieve the boat. Then they took turns crossing in the small boat.

3. What happened to Bombur at the black river crossing?
   He fell in and the spell of the black water took effect on him. He fell asleep and had to be carried.

4. What did Bilbo see from the top of the oak tree in Mirkwood?
   There were sun and wind and butterflies above the canopy–and no end to the forest in sight.

5. Why did the travelers leave the path?
   They were attracted to the lights in the forest, thinking there would be food at a camp fire. They were very hungry.

6. What happened when they entered the ring of light to beg for food?
   It all disappeared.

7. How did Bilbo get separated from the others in Mirkwood?
   When the firelight from the woodland gathering disappeared, he got separated from the others in the darkness and confusion.

8. What made Bilbo feel fierce and bold?
   Bilbo killed a spider and freed himself without the help of a wizard or anyone else.

9. Identify Sting.
   That's the name Bilbo gave his sword after he killed the spider.

10. How did Bilbo rescue the dwarves from the spiders?
    He put on the ring to sneak in and see what was going on. He killed several spiders by throwing stones at them, then he drew them away from their prey (the dwarves) by taunting them. Leaving the spiders astray, he sneaked back to free the dwarves. When the spiders returned, he used Sting to fight them off. He killed many and led others away from the dwarves again. The spiders grew afraid of Sting and eventually gave up the chase.

11. Who was missing after the travelers were rescued from the spiders?
    Thorin was missing.

12. How did Thorin get separated from the others?
    In the circle of light, he fell asleep. The wood elves tied him up and took them to their king.

Chapter 9
1. Why were the travelers actually glad to be captured by the wood elves?
   They were sick and tired and starving. Although they were prisoners, they at least received food and drink.

2. How did Bilbo keep from getting captured by the wood elves?
   He slipped on the ring.

3. How did Bilbo rescue Thorin & Co. from the Elvenking?
   He took the keys to the cells from the drunken guards, freed the others and put them in empty barrels. The empty barrels were unloaded through the trap doors and floated away.

Chapter 10
1. What sight did Bilbo see as he floated along on the barrel-raft?
   He saw Lonely Mountain.

2. How had Bilbo and the travelers been lucky?
   They had come out of Mirkwood on the only route available, the river. The path they had been told to follow had been worn away by floods and earthquakes, so they actually stumbled onto the only exit.

3. What songs did men near Long Lake still sing?
   They sang the tales of the dwarf kings of the Mountain, Thror and Thrain of the race of Durin. They sang of the coming of the dragon and the fall of the Lords of Dale. Some also sang of the return of Thror and Thrain.

4. Why did Thorin demand to be taken to the Master of the Men of the Lake?
   He was there to announce his presence (he was, after all, the descendant of the King of the Mountain about whom the people sang), to get food and rest, and to prepare for his journey to the mountain.

5. Why did the Master allow the travelers to stay, treat them well, and send them to the mountain with provisions?
   He didn't totally believe the legends about the dwarf king, but he didn't want to miss an opportunity to get a portion of the treasure if, in fact, the whole thing was true. Also, the presence of the dwarves was disruptive to daily business, so he gladly gave them provisions and sent them on their way.

Chapter 11
1. Why did the men of the town leave the travelers at the end of the third day?
   They were close to the mountain, and the men were afraid.

2. Identify Ravenhill.
   Ravenhill was a high place on the southwest side of the mountain where an old watch post had been. The travelers made their first camp just below this point.

3. What did the scouting party see at the front gate?
   They saw dark smoke.

4. What were the dwarves looking for on the western side of the mountain?
   They were looking for the secret entrance to the mountain that was shown on the map.

5. How did the dwarves get the secret door open?
   According to the runes on the map, a ray of light would shine on the keyhole at sunset on the last day of autumn. Bilbo vaguely remembered something about that. When it happened, they inserted Thorin's key, and the door opened.

Chapter 12
1. What did Bilbo see at the end of the tunnel?
   He saw Smaug, the dragon, sleeping on piles and piles of treasures.

2. Why did Smaug go into a rage upon awakening?
   He knew the cup had been stolen.

3. Why did Bilbo go back down the tunnel a second time?
   He went to try to find out if Smaug had a weakness.

4. How did Bilbo answer when the dragon asked who he was?
   He answered in riddles, which fascinated the dragon.

5. Which of Smaug's senses was very keen?
   His sense of smell was very keen.

6. What was Smaug's weakness that Bilbo discovered?
   Smaug's soft underbelly was coated with gems, but there was one empty patch in the hollow of his left breast.

7. Why did Thorin tell Bilbo to leave the thrush alone?
   Thrushes were tame to his ancestors. They were a magical and long-lived breed that were sometimes used as messengers. This one could even have been alive at the time of Thorin's grandfather.

8. Why did the dwarves move their camp to within the tunnel?
   Bilbo figured that Smaug would come out that night and destroy everything in the general area where he thought the other end of the tunnel might be. The tunnel seemed like a safer camp for the night.

9. What did Thorin say was the greatest treasure of the Mountain?
   The Arkenstone was. It was a great, white gem like a globe with a thousand facets.

Chapter 13

1. Why did Thorin & Co. go down the tunnel?
   It was their only chance to find another way out after they closed the secret door and couldn't get it open again.

2. What did Bilbo put in his deepest pocket?
   He pocketed the Arkenstone.

3. How did Thorin & Co. get out of the Mountain?
   After they reveled in the treasure, Thorin took them through the Mountain to the place where the Running River began. They followed the water channels to the front gate exit.

4. Where did the travelers go after they got out of the Mountain?
   They went to Ravenhill.

5. Identify "cram."
   It was a biscuit-like food that the Lake men sent in the provisions.

Chapter 14

1. Identify Esgaroth.
    Esgaroth was the name of the town where the Lake Men lived.

2. Identify Bard.
    Bard was a descendant of Girion, Lord of the Dale. Bard killed Smaug with his black arrow.

3. How did Bard know where to aim when he shot Smaug?
    The old thrush told him about Smaug's weakness.

4. What was Bard's reward for killing the dragon?
    The people wanted to make him king. The Master offered to let Bard return to Dale, which was freed by his valor, and to let any who wanted to follow him go.

5. What was Bard's response to the Master's offer?
    He chose, for time being, to remain as a subject of the Master and to help restore Esgaroth after the war with Smaug.

6. Who came to help the Lake people, at Bard's request?
    The Elvenking brought his people to help.

7. Why did all the men of arms go to the Mountain?
    They were seeking the treasure.

Chapter 15

1. Identify Roäc.
    Roäc was a raven, son of Carc, for whom Ravenhill was named. He brought news to the dwarves that Smaug had been killed and that many were seeking the treasure of the Mountain. he warned Thorin not to trust the Master; rather, to trust Bard.

2. What did Thorin ask Roäc to do?
    Thorin asked Roäc to send word to all his scattered kinsmen for them to come to the Mountain.

3. What did Bard ask of Thorin, and what was Thorin's response?
    Bard asked Thorin to share the treasure with those who justly had a right to a portion of it. Thorin refused.

4. What did the messenger from Esgaroth declare?
   He declared the Mountain besieged. The armies would not attack but would not let the dwarves resupply until they agreed to negotiate.

Chapter 16
1. What news did Roäc bring the besieged dwarves?
   Dain and more than 500 dwarves were within two days' march of Dale.

2. Why did Bilbo offer to take Bombur's watch?
   Bilbo wanted to be able to leave undetected.

3. What did Bilbo give Bard? Why?
   Bilbo gave Bard the Arkenstone so Bard could use it in bargaining with Thorin. Bilbo wanted peace.

4. Who praised Bilbo for his meeting with Bard?
   Gandalf did.

Chapter 17
1. Why did Thorin throw Bilbo out of his camp?
   Bilbo confessed that he gave the Arkenstone to Bard.

2. Why wouldn't Bard let Dain and the dwarves pass?
   He could see that they were well supplied and would resupply the dwarves at the Mountain, dragging out the time it would take to make Thorin comply.

3. What announcement did Gandalf make?
   He announced that bats, goblins and wargs had come to fight.

4. What were the armies in The Battle of Five Armies?
   They were armies made of wargs, goblins, dwarves, elves, and men.

5. What plan did Gandalf propose?
   He suggested that they could lure the goblins into the valley between the arms of the Mountain, manning the parts that struck out to the south and east. The elves would be on the southern part and the men and dwarves would be on the eastern section.

6. Why did the dwarves agree to fight with the men and elves against the goblins and wargs?
   It was their only chance for survival.

7. Who were the first to charge against the goblins?
    The elves were, followed by Dain's dwarves.

8. When all seemed lost against the goblins, what appeared on the scene?
    The eagles came to help.

9. What happened to Bilbo during the battle?
    He put on his ring to become invisible, but he was still struck in the head with a stone and was knocked out.

Chapter 18

1. When Bilbo awoke after being knocked out by the stone, what did he see?
    It looked as if the battle had ended and the goblins had been defeated.

2. Why did Thorin call for Bilbo?
    He wanted to make peace with Bilbo before he died.

3. What did Bilbo miss at the end of the battle while he was knocked out?
    The eagles fought against the goblins. Beorn came and fought, found Thorin wounded and carried him to safety, returned tot he battle and killed Bolg, the goblin king. With Bolg dead, many goblins fled. They scattered and were killed by the elves and the armies who drove them away. Some goblins were eliminated by the perils of Mirkwood.

4. What parting gift did Bard bestow upon Thorin?
    he placed the Arkenstone on his breast at his burial.

5. What parting gift did the Elvenking give Thorin?
    He laid Orcrist upon Thorin's tomb.

6. Who led the dwarves after Thorin's death?
    Dain did.

7. What did Dain give Bard? Why?
    He gave Bard 1/14 of the treasure, as Thorin had promised him for the Arkenstone.

8. What did Bard do with his riches?
    He rewarded the Master of the Lake people, the Elvenking and Bilbo.

9. What did Bilbo give the Elvenking? Why?
    he gave him a necklace of silver and pearls to repay his hospitality.

10. Who became a great chief, ruling lands between the mountains and the wood?
    Beorn did.

Chapter 19

1. Where had Gandalf been while he was away from Thorin and Co.?
   He was at a council of wizards of good magic, who drove the Necromancer from his hold on the south of Mirkwood.

2. What did Gandalf and Bilbo dig up?
   They dug up the troll treasure.

3. When Bilbo arrived home, what did he find?
   His belongings were being auctioned. He was presumed dead.

4. What, besides spoons, did Bilbo lose?
   He lost his reputation. He was an elf-friend, had the honor of dwarves and wizards, and was no longer quite respectable among the hobbits.

5. Who came to visit Bilbo a few years after his return home?
   Gandalf and Balin came.

6. What news did Balin bring?
   He said that the land of the Mountain was quite prosperous and all was well.

7. What were Gandalf's last words to Bilbo in this book?
   ". . . Surely you don't disbelieve the prophecies, because you had a hand in bringing them about yourself? You don't really suppose, do you, that all your adventures and escapes were managed by mere luck, just for your sole benefit? You are a very fine person, Mr. Baggins, and I am very fond of you; but you are only quite a little fellow in a wide world after all."

MULTIPLE CHOICE FORMAT STUDY GUIDE/QUIZ QUESTIONS - *The Hobbit*

<u>Chapter 1</u>
1. Which is NOT a characteristic of a hobbit:
    a. love to eat
    b. no beards
    c. love adventure
    d. no magic

2. Identify as **H**obbit, **D**warf, or **W**izard:
    ___ a. Belladonna Took
    ___ b. Dwalin
    ___ c. Bungo Baggins
    ___ d. Gandalf
    ___ e. Thorin
    ___ f. Bombur
    ___ g. Bilbo
    ___ h. Dori

3. What was unusual about the Tooks?
    a. They didn't like to eat.
    b. They were adventurous.
    c. They had magical powers.
    d. b & c

4. Why did Gandalf visit Bilbo Baggins?
    a. To tell him of an adventure he had planned
    b. To drink tea
    c. To see if he would be suitable as a burglar
    d. To borrow some tobacco

5. Who was Bilbo expecting for tea?
    a. Thorin
    b. Balin
    c. His family
    d. Gandalf

6. What about his uninvited guests irked Bilbo?
    a. They filled his home with smoke from their pipes.
    b. They fought with each other.
    c. Their music was too loud.
    d. They made themselves right at home and ordered food and drinks.

Hobbit Multiple Choice Study Questions Chapter 1 Page 2

7. What effect did the dwarves' singing have on Bilbo?
    a. It made him sleepy.
    b. It gave him a headache.
    c. It made him feel adventurous.
    d. It irked him.

8. Gloin thought Bilbo Baggins was
    a. a coward
    b. a good thief
    c. a liar
    d. a wizard

9. Gandalf showed the dwarves something that belonged to Thorin's grandfather. What?
    a. a sword
    b. a pipe
    c. a map
    d. a wooden trunk

10. Identify Dale.
    a. Thorin's grandfather
    b. a town in the shadow of the mountain
    c. Thorin's father
    d. Bilbo's grandfather who lived near the mountain

11. Identify Smaug.
    a. the mist that settled in the mountain valley
    b. Thorin's grandfather
    c. the name of Gandalf's staff
    d. the dragon who lives in the mountain

12. What story did Thorin tell Bilbo?
    a. how his grandfather's kingdom was destroyed
    b. how he got the map and key
    c. how the dwarves beat Smaug
    d. how Gandalf helped the dwarves

13. How did Gandalf get the map and key?
    a. He took it from Smaug.
    b. He took it from Thorin.
    c. Thorin gave it to him.
    d. Thorin's father gave it to him.

Hobbit Multiple Choice Study Questions Chapter 2

<u>Chapter 2</u>
1. Why did Bilbo leave his Hill in such a hurry to go to the Green Dragon Inn?
    a. He was late for a meeting with Gandalf.
    b. His house was full of uninvited dwarves. He went to the inn to get away from them.
    c. Gandalf put a spell on him.
    d. He was late for a meeting with the dwarves.

2. What had Bilbo forgotten to bring with him, and how was it remedied?
    a. He forgot his staff. Gandalf brought it to him.
    b. He forgot his cloak and all provisions. The dwarves provided what he needed, and Gandalf brought a few things from Bilbo's home.
    c. He forgot the map. Dwalin went back to get it.
    d. all of the above

3. When did Bilbo first wish that he were back home?
    a. as soon as he got to the Green Dragon Inn
    b. when they got to the Lone-lands, the weather turned bad, and he was tired
    c. when they met the trolls
    d. when they discovered Gandalf was missing

4. Identify William, Bert and Tom.
    a. They were three of the dwarves.
    b. They were three elves.
    c. They were three wizards.
    d. They were three trolls.

5. What did William catch Bilbo doing?
    a. Bilbo was trying to pick William's pocket.
    b. Bilbo was stealing food.
    c. Bilbo was trying to take some treasure.
    d. Bilbo was stealing the swords.

6. Who saved Bilbo, Thorin and company?
    a. some elves
    b. Bilbo
    c. Gandalf
    d. Thorin

7. What did Gandalf, Thorin, and Bilbo take from the trolls' cave?
    a. weapons
    b. provisions
    c. treasure
    d. all of the above

Hobbit Multiple Choice Study Questions Chapter 3

Chapter 3
1. What kind of creatures inhabited the valley of Rivendell and helped the travelers find the Last Homely Home? What did Bilbo and the dwarves think of them?
    a. elves
    b. trolls
    c. dwarves
    d. hobbits

2. Identify Elrond.
    a. dwarf who helped Bilbo
    b. elf king
    c. town where elves lived
    d. name of the Last Homely Home

3. What important information did Elrond give the travelers?
    a. He told them not to trust Gandalf.
    b. He told them how to defeat the dragon.
    c. He read the moon letters to reveal the way to open a secret door in the Mountain.
    d. He gave them a special rune to cast a spell on the dragon.

4. What was Durin's Day?
    a. name of the day the dragon defeated the dwarves
    b. name of the elves' New Year's Day
    c. name of the day the King of the Mountain died
    d. name of the day the elves celebrated their king

Hobbit Multiple Choice Study Questions Chapter 4

<u>Chapter 4</u>
1. Why did the travelers go into the cave?
    a. to look for goblins
    b. to look for food
    c. to seek shelter from a storm
    d. all of the above

2. What did Bilbo dream in the cave?
    a. that he was home drinking tea
    b. that a crack in the wall got bigger and the floor gave way
    c. that a dragon came through the crack in the wall
    d. that he was in a terrible storm and couldn't get home

3. Bilbo and Thorin & Co. had a nasty surprise in the cave. What was it?
    a. bats attacked them
    b. trolls attacked them
    c. elves attacked them
    d. goblins attacked them

4. Did the goblins get Gandalf?
    a. Yes, but he escaped.
    b. No
    c. Yes
    d. They cast a spell on him but didn't take him with the others.

5. Which is NOT a characteristic of goblins?
    a. bad-hearted
    b. cruel
    c. liked dwarves
    d. made no beautiful things

6. What caused the Great Goblin to become enraged?
    a. Gandalf's wizardry
    b. Bilbo asked for food.
    c. The dwarves tried to escape.
    d. He saw Thorin's sword.

Hobbit Multiple Choice Study Questions Chapter 4 Continued

7. How did the travelers escape from the Goblins' cavern?
    a. Gandalf made the fire blow up, which burned the goblins. The dwarves escaped in the confusion.
    b. The goblins foolishly left them unguarded for a short time, and the travelers made the most of the opportunity.
    c. Gandalf cast a spell which made the goblins all fall asleep. The travelers then fled.
    d. The travelers outwitted the goblins in a game of riddles.

8. Identify Biter and Beater.
    a. They were cousins of Dwalin and Balin.
    b. They were friends with Oin and Gloin.
    c. They were goblin names for Orcrist and Glamdring.
    d. They were goblins names for Thorin and Gandalf.

9. Goblins run faster than dwarves. How did the travelers escape the pursuit of the goblins?
    a. They went in underground tunnels too small for the goblins.
    b. Thorin and Gandalf turned and used their swords to kill many goblins. The rest ran in fear.
    c. They hid among the trees.
    d. The goblins gave up for no apparent reason, much to the surprise of the travelers.

10. What happened to Dori and Bilbo?
    a. Sneaky goblins grabbed Dori from behind. Bilbo fell and hit his head.
    b. Dori tripped on a rock. Bilbo fell and hit his head on the rock.
    c. Dori couldn't run as fast as the other dwarves with Bilbo on his back; so they got separated from the others.
    d. The goblins grabbed them and took them both back to the cave.

Hobbit Multiple Choice Study Questions Chapter 5

Chapter 5
1. When Bilbo awoke after falling off of Dori's shoulders when the goblins grabbed Dori, what was strange about his surroundings?
    a. He was under water.
    b. He was covered in slime.
    c. He was in complete darkness.
    d. He was surrounded by many unusual dark shapes.

2. While groping around on the floor, what did Bilbo find and put in his pocket?
    a. He found a ring.
    b. He found a rock.
    c. He found a key.
    d. He found a stick.

3. How did Bilbo know his knife was an elvish blade, too?
    a. It had the elf insignia engraved on it.
    b. The elf who gave it to him told him so.
    c. The handle was carved with a goblin on it.
    d. It glowed.

4. Identify Gollum.
    a. Bilbo's knife
    b. Goblin who captured Bilbo
    c. Sometimes man, sometimes bear
    d. Small, slimy, water creature with big pale eyes who called himself "precious"

5. Gollum and Bilbo made a deal. What was it?
    a. Bilbo would give Gollum the key in exchange for his freedom.
    b. Bilbo would give Gollum the ring in exchange for his freedom.
    c. The winner of the riddle game would get what he wanted from the other.
    d. If Bilbo lost the riddle game, he would give Gollum his birthday present.

6. How did Bilbo win the riddle game with Gollum?
    a. Gollum didn't know what was in Bilbo's pockets.
    b. He had good luck.
    c. He pretended to be braver than he felt.
    d. All of the above.

Hobbit Multiple Choice Study Questions Chapter 5 Continued

7. Where was Gollum's lost birthday present?
    a. Lost in the water
    b. In Bilbo's pocket
    c. Under a rock
    d. The goblins got it.

8. How did Bilbo discover the power of the ring?
    a. Gollum told him, as a part of their agreement.
    b. He overheard the goblins talking about the powers of the ring.
    c. After he slipped it on his finger, Gollum passed right by him as if he were invisible.
    d. There was an inscription on the ring warning the wearer that although the wearer would be invisible, his shadow could still be seen.

9. How did Bilbo find the way out of Gollum's land?
    a. He simply followed Gollum to the exit.
    b. Gollum took him there as a part of their agreement.
    c. The ring led him there.
    d. He used the glowing of his knife to help him find his way, since he knew goblins were near the exit.

10. Why didn't Bilbo kill Gollum?
    a. Bilbo felt sorry for Gollum.
    b. Gollum had been kind to Bilbo.
    c. If Bilbo had killed Gollum, the powers of the ring would have ended.
    d. He tried but failed.

11. What gave Bilbo away to the goblins as he tried to escape out the door?
    a. He sneezed.
    b. His knife glowed.
    c. His shadow gave him away.
    d. The ring slipped off his finger causing him to become visible again.

12. Why did the goblins give up looking for Bilbo?
    a. They got hungry and went back to the cave for lunch.
    b. They were afraid of his knife.
    c. Gandalf appeared.
    d. The sunshine made their legs wobble and their heads giddy.

Hobbit Multiple Choice Study Questions Chapter 6

Chapter 6
1. Why did the dwarves have a better opinion of Bilbo Baggins when he rejoined them after his adventures with Gollum and the goblins?
    a. They missed him while he was gone and realized how much help he had been to them.
    b. After he told them of his adventures, they thought he was clever, brave, and a good burglar after all.
    c. Gandalf finally made them realize Bilbo's value.
    d. All of the above.

2. What detail about his adventures with Gollum did Bilbo leave out when he told the dwarves the story?
    a. He didn't tell them about the riddles.
    b. He didn't tell them about Gollum.
    c. He didn't tell them about the ring.
    d. He didn't tell them about the birthday present he gave Gollum.

3. Where were the travelers after the goblin adventures?
    a. They were at the Green Dragon Inn.
    b. They were in the Lone-lands.
    c. They were in the valley of Rivendell.
    d. They were through the Misty Mountains.

4. Why did the travelers climb up into the trees?
    a. To escape from the elves
    b. To escape from the goblins
    c. To escape from the wolves
    d. To escape from the eagles

5. Who saved Bilbo from the wolves?
    a. Dori
    b. Gandalf
    c. The Wargs
    d. Thorin

6. Identify wargs.
    a. wolf-friends of the goblins
    b. eagle-friends of the dwarves
    c. goblin-friends of the elves
    d. elf-friends of the wolves

Hobbit Multiple Choice Study Questions Chapter 6 Continued

7. Why were the wargs at the clearing?
    a. They were waiting to ambush the travelers.
    b. They were waiting to fight the eagles.
    c. They were waiting to meet the goblins.
    d. They were waiting for the rest of the wargs to come.

8. How did Gandalf try to get rid of the wargs and goblins?
    a. He brought bright sunshine upon the land.
    b. He showed them the glow of his sword.
    c. He lit pine cones on fire and threw them at the wargs and goblins.
    d. All of the above

9. Who or what saved the travelers from the wargs, goblins, and fire?
    a. Gandalf's plan worked.
    b. The eagles came and rescued the travelers.
    c. The bright sunlight forced the wargs and goblins back into the darkness, and the travelers were then able to escape from the fire.
    d. Bilbo summoned all of his courage, put on the ring, and went right through all of the wargs and goblins to go get help from Elrond.

Hobbit Multiple Choice Study Questions Chapter 7

Chapter 7
1. Identify Beorn.
   a. bear-man
   b. elvenking
   c. eagle king
   d. goblin leader

2. Why did Gandalf introduce the dwarves a few at a time to Beorn?
   a. That's just how they happened to come along.
   b. Beorn was a small and timid man; so many visitors at once would have frightened him.
   c. It was Gandalf's way of getting Beorn's acceptance of the whole group.
   d. Beorn's house was very small; all of the dwarves would not have fit in it at one time.

3. What news did Gandalf bring the dwarves about Beorn's whereabouts?
   a. Beorn had gone to fight the wargs.
   b. Beorn had gone to check out their story.
   c. Beorn had gone hunting for dinner.
   d. Beorn had gone looking for his ponies.

4. Beorn warned them about some things in Mirkwood. What?
   a. Not to touch or drink the water from the black river
   b. Not to leave the path
   c. Not to eat the purple berries
   d. a & b only

5. How do we know Beorn liked the travelers?
   a. He gave them food & lodging, lent them his ponies, and watched after them.
   b. He didn't eat them.
   c. He told Gandalf how fond he was of them.
   d. All of the above

6. Why did Gandalf leave Thorin & Co.?
   a. He wanted to see if they could make it on their own.
   b. He had pressing business elsewhere.
   c. They made him angry with their bickering and complaining.
   d. All of the above

Hobbit Multiple Choice Study Questions Chapter 7 Continued

7. What were Gandalf's parting words to the travelers as he left them at Mirkwood?
    a. "I don't care if you sniveling complainers *ever* come out alive!"
    b. "May you walk with the sure-footedness of a goat, the heart of a lion, and have the best of luck on your journey."
    c. "Don't leave the path."
    d. "I'll see you at the Mountain!"

Hobbit Multiple Choice Study Questions Chapter 8

<u>Chapter 8</u>
1. Describe Mirkwood.
    a. It was like a paradise.
    b. It was dark and scary.
    c. It was full of hills and craggy rocks.
    d. It was desert-like.

2. How did the travelers cross the black water?
    a. They walked through it.
    b. They rode the ponies through it.
    c. They swam.
    d. They used a boat.

3. What happened to Bombur at the black river crossing?
    a. He drowned.
    b. He fell in and became enchanted.
    c. He got kicked in the head by a deer.
    d. He began to see hallucinations.

4. What did Bilbo see from the top of the oak tree in Mirkwood?
    a. Gandalf
    b. More trees
    c. Eagles
    d. Goblins

5. Why did the travelers leave the path?
    a. They thought there would be food where the lights were.
    b. They became mesmerized and enchanted by the lights and were drawn towards them.
    c. They were frightened in the forest and were seeking companionship.
    d. They were trying to follow the deer to fresh water.

6. What happened when they entered the ring of light to beg for food?
    a. They were no longer hungry.
    b. They were magically transported out of the forest.
    c. Everything disappeared and they were in darkness.
    d. They found that the light was caused by a gathering of firefly faeries.

Hobbit Multiple Choice Study Questions Chapter 8 Continued

7. How did Bilbo get separated from the others in Mirkwood?
    a. He decided he could do better on his own and left them.
    b. He went for help.
    c. He got separated from them by mistake in the darkness and confusion.
    d. The others were angry with him and left him.

8. What made Bilbo feel fierce and bold?
    a. His hunger gave him more courage than he normally would have had.
    b. He was sick and tired of everyone complaining about him and decided to show them that they were wrong.
    c. The cover of darkness gave him courage.
    d. He had killed the spider and freed himself without help from anyone else.

9. Identify Sting.
    a. Spider leader
    b. Bilbo's knife
    c. Spider poison
    d. Code name for Bilbo's operation to free the dwarves

10. How did Bilbo rescue the dwarves from the spiders?
    a. He freed them while the spiders slept.
    b. He cleverly poisoned the spiders with their own venom.
    c. He led them away on a wild goose chase, sneaked back in to free the dwarves, and killed many spiders with his knife.
    d. He tricked the goblins into fighting the spiders and freed the dwarves in the confusion.

11. Who was missing after the travelers were rescued from the spiders?
    a. Dori
    b. Bilbo
    c. Gandalf
    d. Thorin

12. How did Thorin get separated from the others?
    a. Because he was the leader of the group, the spiders put him in a separate cell.
    b. Woodelves carried him away.
    c. He got lost in the darkness.
    d. Bilbo forgot to free him; he thought he had everyone, but he didn't.

Hobbit Multiple Choice Study Questions Chapter 9

<u>Chapter 9</u>
1. How did the travelers feel about being captured by the wood elves?
    a. They were angry at their own stupidity for being captured.
    b. They were very concerned about the further delay in their journey.
    c. They were afraid the wood elves would eat them before they could escape.
    d. They were relieved to at least have food and shelter.

2. How did Bilbo keep from getting captured by the wood elves?
    a. He slipped on the ring and became invisible.
    b. He hid in a barrel.
    c. He disguised himself as a wood elf.
    d. He was almost captured but escaped in some confusion and was never missed.

3. How did Bilbo rescue Thorin & Co. from the Elvenking?
    a. He made a deal with the Elvenking, offering him part of the riches of the mountain if he would release them to go on their journey.
    b. He loaded them into barrels and sent them floating down the river.
    c. He got the keys from the drunken guards and led his friends out a secret pathway he found in the woods.
    d. He dressed them in the clothing of the drunken guards, and they were not noticed as they walked right out of the Elvenking's domain.

Hobbit Multiple Choice Study Questions Chapter 10

Chapter 10
1. What sight did Bilbo see as he floated along on the barrel-raft?
    a. He saw Smaug.
    b. He saw Gandalf with some other travelers.
    c. He saw Lonely Mountain.
    d. He saw the Elvenking.

2. How had Bilbo and the travelers been lucky?
    a. By chance, they had made it out of Mirkwood by the only route available–the river.
    b. In being captured, they had actually been saved.
    c. They weren't seriously injured or drowned in the river.
    d. All of the above.

3. What songs did men near Long Lake still sing?
    a. They sang lullabies.
    b. They sang of the fall of the Lords of Dale and the return of the King of the Mountain.
    c. They sang the war song of Smaug, the dragon.
    d. They sang of the earthquakes and floods that destroyed the King of the Mountain.

4. Why did Thorin demand to be taken to the Master of the Men of the Lake?
    a. He wanted to announce his presence, get food and rest, and prepare for his journey to the mountain.
    b. He wanted to thank him for saving them from the Elvenking.
    c. He wanted to see how many guards the Master had.
    d. He wanted to see the man who had so many loyal and loving subjects.

5. Why did the Master treat the travelers well, and send them to the mountain with provisions?
    a. He was afraid Smaug would attack if he did not treat them well.
    b. He was just a wonderful person and a wonderful host; it was his nature to be kind and giving to strangers.
    c. He wanted a share of the treasure if, in fact, it did exist.
    d. He was afraid of them.

Hobbit Multiple Choice Study Questions Chapter 11

Chapter 11
1. Why did the men of the town leave the travelers at the end of the third day?
    a. They only had three days' of provisions.
    b. They became frightened when they got so close to the mountain.
    c. They were only paid to travel for three days.
    d. They were sick of Thorin's ungrateful and pompous attitude.

2. Identify Ravenhill.
    a. The Lord of the Mountain
    b. Place where Smaug lived
    c. Point where the men of the town left Thorin & Co.
    d. Site of an old watch post on the south side of the mountain.

3. What did the scouting party see at the front gate?
    a. Treasure
    b. Bones
    c. Dark smoke
    d. Smaug

4. What were the dwarves looking for on the western side of the mountain?
    a. Smaug
    b. Treasure
    c. A secret door
    d. Food

5. How did the dwarves get the secret door open?
    a. Bilbo's ring opened it.
    b. A ray of the setting sun shone on the keyhole, and they used Thorin's key to enter.
    c. They tied a rope to it and used their ponies to pull it open.
    d. Bilbo remembered and spoke the spell that would open the door.

Hobbit Multiple Choice Study Questions Chapter 12

Chapter 12

1. What did Bilbo see at the end of the tunnel?
    a. Smaug lying on a huge pile of treasure
    b. The ghost of Thorin's father, the King of the Mountain
    c. Huge wooden doors leading into a great chamber
    d. A warning sign that said, "Beware of the Dragon!"

2. Why did Smaug go into a rage upon awakening?
    a. He was always in a rage upon awakening. He always woke up grumpy.
    b. He knew a cup had been stolen.
    c. He felt a jewel missing from his breast.
    d. He was frightened of the unknown smell of Bilbo.

3. Why did Bilbo go back down the tunnel a second time?
    a. To find the Arkenstone
    b. To find another exit
    c. To find if Smaug had a weakness
    d. To find food

4. How did Bilbo answer when the dragon asked who he was?
    a. He answered in riddles, which fascinated the dragon.
    b. He told Smaug it was none of his business.
    c. He replied that he was "the twin of death, the end of the dragon, and the bearer of riches untold."
    d. He talked into the cup to disguise his voice and to make himself sound bigger than he was.

5. Which of Smaug's senses was very keen?
    a. Sight
    b. Smell
    c. Hearing
    d. Taste

6. What was Smaug's weakness that Bilbo discovered?
    a. He loved gold.
    b. He had a temper.
    c. His breast armor was missing a jewel.
    d. He couldn't resist bantering in riddles.

Hobbit Multiple Choice Study Questions Chapter 12 Continued

7. Why did Thorin tell Bilbo to leave the thrush alone?
    a. Thorin was carried away with bossing everybody about everything.
    b. Bilbo was using it as target practice, and Thorin thought that was too cruel.
    c. The thrush was a very good friend of his.
    d. This thrush could have been alive at the time of Thorin's grandfather, a time when the thrushes were a tame and magical breed.

8. Why did the dwarves move their camp to within the tunnel?
    a. To be closer to Smaug so that they could better watch him
    b. To get out of the weather
    c. To avoid being destroyed by Smaug
    d. To have easier access for exploring the cave

9. What did Thorin say was the greatest treasure of the Mountain?
    a. The Arkenstone
    b. The water within
    c. Smaug
    d. The memories of his ancestors

Hobbit Multiple Choice Study Questions Chapter 13

Chapter 13
1. Why did Thorin & Co. go down the tunnel?
    a. to find the Arkenstone
    b. to find a way out
    c. to find Smaug
    d. to find water

2. What did Bilbo put in his deepest pocket?
    a. the Arkenstone
    b. the map
    c. his knife
    d. extra food

3. How did Thorin & Co. get out of the Mountain?
    a. They followed Smaug's trail.
    b. They followed a secret tunnel.
    c. They followed the raven.
    d. They followed the river.

4. Where did the travelers go after they got out of the Mountain?
    a. Esgaroth
    b. Ravenhill
    c. Mirkwood
    d. Misty Mountains

5. Identify "cram."
    a. It's what the dwarves did with the treasure. They crammed it in their pockets.
    b. It's the word for Smaug's bejeweled underbelly because it was crammed with jewels.
    c. It's a biscuit-like food.
    d. It's an ancient type of weapon the dwarves found in the mountain.

Hobbit Multiple Choice Study Questions Chapter 14

<u>Chapter 14</u>
1. Identify Esgaroth.
    a. He killed Smaug.
    b. He was the master of the lake people.
    c. It was the name of the town where the lake people lived.
    d. He was the Elvenking.

2. Identify Bard.
    a. He killed Smaug.
    b. He was the master of the lake people.
    c. It was the name of the town where the lake people lived.
    d. He was the Elvenking.

3. How did the archer know where to aim when he shot Smaug?
    a. He aimed for the neck, thinking it would be the most vulnerable spot.
    b. He had killed a few dragons before.
    c. Bilbo had slipped into the town and told him.
    d. The thrush told him.

4. What was Bard's reward for killing the dragon?
    a. He received the jewels from the dragon's belly.
    b. The master offered to let him return to Dale and let go anyone who wanted to follow him.
    c. Bilbo gave him the Arkenstone.
    d. He was made king of the lake people.

5. What did Bard do after killing the dragon?
    a. He left the lake town and went to the dale.
    b. He stayed in the lake town to help restore it.
    c. He left, but no one ever knew where he went.
    d. He left the lake town and continued on his quest.

6. Who came to help the Lake people, at Bard's request?
    a. the eagles
    b. Roäc
    c. Beorn
    d. the Elvenking

Hobbit Multiple Choice Study Questions Chapter 14 Continued

7. Why did all the men of arms go to the Mountain?
   a. to find the King of the Mountain
   b. to look at Smaug's lair
   c. to make sure there were no other dragons
   d. to find the treasure

Hobbit Multiple Choice Study Questions Chapter 15

<u>Chapter 15</u>
1. Which is NOT true about Roäc.
    a. Ravenhill was named for him.
    b. He brought news of Smaug's death to the dwarves.
    c. He warned Thorin not to trust the master of the people; rather, to trust Bard.
    d. He told Thorin that many were seeking the treasure of the mountain.

2. What did Thorin ask Roäc to do?
    a. gather the eagles for battle
    b. send word to Bard that he would receive his fair share of the treasure
    c. send word to his scattered kinsmen to come to the mountain
    d. give a signal when the men were within striking distance

3. What did Bard ask of Thorin, and what was Thorin's response?
    a. Bard asked Thorin to help fight the goblins & wargs; Thorin refused.
    b. Bard asked Thorin to give him all the treasure; Thorin refused.
    c. Bard asked Thorin to give him a share of the treasure; Thorin agreed.
    d. Bard asked Thorin to share the treasure with those who deserved it; Thorin refused.

4. What did the messenger from Esgaroth declare?
    a. He said that the goblins were coming.
    b. He said that the lake town men were coming to take the treasure.
    c. He said that the mountain was besieged.
    d. He said that Thorin must surrender.

Hobbit Multiple Choice Study Questions Chapter 16

Chapter 16
1. What news did Roäc bring the besieged dwarves?
    a. The goblins and wargs were coming.
    b. The lake men were coming.
    c. Dain & more than 500 dwarves were coming.
    d. The Elvenking was ready to attack.

2. Why did Bilbo offer to take Bombur's watch?
    a. If he were on watch, he could leave without being detected.
    b. He knew Bombur was very, very tired and thought he'd do him a favor.
    c. Thorin wanted to talk to Bombur, so he sent Bilbo as relief.
    d. It was making so much noise that Bombur thought it would give away his position. Bilbo took the watch to put it deep in his pocket where it would not be heard.

3. What did Bilbo give Bard? Why?
    a. Bilbo gave Bard directions about how to best defeat the dwarves because he knew others deserved part of the treasure.
    b. Bilbo gave Bard the map and key to the secret entrance to the mountain so the men could sneak in, take the dwarves by surprise and overcome them without a big battle. Bilbo wanted as few casualties as possible in resolving the situation.
    c. Bilbo gave Bard the Arkenstone so he could use it in bargaining with Thorin because Bilbo wanted peace.
    d. Bilbo knew that Thorin had made a wrong decision, so he gave Bard his allegiance, promising to help him in any way he could.

4. Who praised Bilbo for his meeting with Bard?
    a. Thorin
    b. Gandalf
    c. Roac
    d. Bombur

Hobbit Multiple Choice Study Questions Chapter 17

<u>Chapter 17</u>
1. Why did Thorin throw Bilbo out of his camp?
    a. He found out that Bilbo left camp while on watch.
    b. He found out that Bilbo had promised his allegiance to Bard.
    c. He found out that Bilbo had given the Arkenstone to Bard.
    d. Bilbo and Thorin got into an argument, and Thorin got so mad he threw Bilbo out.

2. Why wouldn't Bard let Dain and the dwarves pass?
    a. It wasn't safe.
    b. He didn't want them to resupply the dwarves.
    c. He wanted all the treasure for himself.
    d. He couldn't; there wasn't enough room.

3. What announcement did Gandalf make?
    a. Bats, goblins, and wargs had come to fight.
    b. Thorin had to give up the treasure.
    c. He would not take sides in the fight.
    d. No one would win the battle.

4. Which was not an army in The Battle of Five Armies?
    a. bats
    b. goblins
    c. men
    d. ravens

5. What plan did Gandalf propose?
    a. Lure the goblins into the valley between the arms of the mountain, manning the spurs that struck out to the south and east; elves on the south and dwarves on the east.
    b. Lure the goblins into the valley between the arms of the mountain and set fire to the valley in several different places, trapping and killing all of the goblins and their accomplices.
    c. Men, elves, and dwarves should all join together to defend the fortress at the mountain, using the fortifications already in place for defense.
    d. Place Smaug's body at the front gate of the mountain, make fire and smoke and noise to simulate Smaug's presence. Have Roac send word to the goblins that Smaug is not dead–so the goblins will retreat.

Hobbit Multiple Choice Study Questions Chapter 17 Continued

6. Why did the dwarves agree to fight with the men and elves against the goblins and wargs?
    a. The men and elves told them they could keep their treasure if they would just help them fight against the goblins.
    b. They were trapped between the two sides and had to choose one way or another to fight.
    c. It was their only chance to survive.
    d. All of the above

7. Who were the first to charge against the goblins?
    a. elves
    b. dwarves
    c. men

8. When all seemed lost against the goblins, who/what appeared on the scene?
    a. Gandalf
    b. Beorn
    c. Faeries
    d. Eagles

9. What happened to Bilbo during the battle?
    a. He was killed.
    b. He was captured by the goblins.
    c. He was cornered by wargs.
    d. He was knocked unconscious.

Hobbit Multiple Choice Study Questions Chapter 18

<u>Chapter 18</u>
1. When Bilbo awoke after being knocked out by the stone, what did he see?
    a. The battle was still raging.
    b. He could only see goblins and wargs–no one else.
    c. It looked as if the battle had ended and the goblins had been defeated.
    d. Thorin and Gandalf were standing over him.

2. Why did Thorin call for Bilbo?
    a. He wanted to make peace with Bilbo before he died.
    b. He wanted to appoint him leader of the dwarves before he died.
    c. He wanted to give Bilbo the Arkenstone in remembrance of their adventure.
    d. All of the above.

3. What did Bilbo miss at the end of the battle while he was knocked out?
    a. The eagles and Beorn came to fight against the goblins.
    b. Beorn found Thorin wounded and carried him to safety.
    c. Beorn killed Bolg, and many of the goblins then fled.
    d. All of the above.

4. What parting gift did Bard bestow upon Thorin?
    a. the title "King of the Mountain"
    b. the Arkenstone
    c. a king's tribute
    d. all of the above

5. What parting gift did the Elvenking give Thorin?
    a. the Arkenstone
    b. the title "King of the Mountain"
    c. Orcrist
    d. all of the above

6. Who led the dwarves after Thorin's death?
    a. Bilbo
    b. Bard
    c. Gandalf
    d. Dain

Hobbit Multiple Choice Study Questions Chapter 18 Continued

7. What did Dain give Bard?
   a. Orcrist
   b. 1/14th of the treasure
   c. the jewels from Smaug's belly
   d. the Arkenstone

8. What did Bard do with his riches?
   a. rewarded the Master of the Lake
   b. rewarded the Elvenking
   c. rewarded Bilbo
   d. all of the above

9. What did Bilbo give the Elvenking? Why?
   a. the cup he originally took from Smaug
   b. the Arkenstone
   c. a necklace
   d. the jewels from Smaug's belly

10. Who became a great chief, ruling lands between the mountains and the wood?
    a. Dain
    b. Bard
    c. Beorn
    d. Bilbo

Hobbit Multiple Choice Study Questions Chapter 19

Chapter 19

1. Where had Gandalf been while he was away from Thorin and Co.?
    a. at a council of wizards
    b. in the south of Mirkwood
    c. driving the Necromancer from Mirkwood
    d. all of the above

2. What did Gandalf and Bilbo dig up?
    a. treasure from the trolls
    b. Thorin's body
    c. roots to eat
    d. treasure forgotten in the mountain

3. When Bilbo arrived home, what did he find?
    a. Everything was just as he had left it.
    b. His belongings were being auctioned, and he was presumed dead.
    c. Gandalf was waiting for him there.
    d. His whole adventure had just been a dream.

4. What, besides spoons, did Bilbo lose?
    a. his pipe
    b. his handkerchiefs
    c. his reputation
    d. his fortune

5. Who came to visit Bilbo a few years after his return home?
    a. Dain
    b. Balin
    c. Gandalf & Balin
    d. Gandalf

6. What news did Balin bring?
    a. The men of the lake were attacking the mountain to get the treasure.
    b. All was well; the land of the mountain was quiet and prosperous.
    c. Bard had died.
    d. Dain had appointed him as the next leader of the dwarves.

Hobbit Multiple Choice Study Questions Chapter 19 Continued

7. What were Gandalf's last words to Bilbo in this book?
   a. "You don't really suppose, do you, that all your adventures and escapes were managed by mere luck, just for your sole benefit? You are a very fine person, Mr. Baggins, and I am very fond of you; but you are only quite a little fellow in a wide world after all!"
   b. "I sent you on this adventure. It was very amusing for me, very good for you–and profitable too. You have learned to believe in yourself and have become quite a hero to the small folk. Old Took would be proud."
   c. "How do you think you managed through this adventure, Mr. Baggins? Just by luck? By chance? No, I think not. Nor did you rise to the occasion on your own, Bilbo. I was there the whole time, helping you, guiding you, keeping you safe. I promised Old Took I would let no harm come to you, and I have kept that promise."
   d. "My dear Bilbo Baggins, the adventure of treasure and Smaug and dwarves having come to an end, I beseech you to consider the greatness to which you have come through this quest and to use that greatness to the best advantage. Come with me to help others as you helped the dwarves, and we will be off on another adventure before a fortnight passes."

ANSWER KEY - MULTIPLE CHOICE STUDY/QUIZ QUESTIONS
The Hobbit

Chapter 1	Chapter 2	Chapter 3	Chapter 4	Chapter 5
1. C	1. D	1. A	1. C	1. C
2. H, D, H, W, D, D, H, D	2. B	2. B	2. B	2. A
3. B	3. B	3. C	3. D	3. D
4. A	4. D	4. B	4. B	4. D
5. D	5. A		5. C	5. C
6. D	6. C		6. D	6. D
7. C	7. A		7. A	7. B
8. A			8. C	8. C
9. C			9. B	9. A
10. B			10. A	10. A
11. D				11. C
12. A				12. D
13. D				

Chapter 6	Chapter 7	Chapter 8	Chapter 9	Chapter 10	Chapter 11
1. B	1. A	1. B	1. D	1. C	1. B
2. C	2. C	2. D	2. A	2. D	2. D
3. D	3. B	3. B	3. B	3. B	3. C
4. C	4. D	4. B		4. A	4. C
5. A	5. A	5. A		5. C	5. B
6. A	6. B	6. C			
7. C	7. C	7. C			
8. C		8. D			
9. B		9. B			
		10. C			
		11. D			
		12. B			

Hobbit Multiple Choice Study/Quiz Question Answer Key Continued

Chapter 12	Chapter 13	Chapter 14	Chapter 15	Chapter 16	Chapter 17
1. A	1. B	1. C	1. D	1. C	1. C
2. B	2. A	2. A	2. C	2. A	2. B
3. C	3. D	3. D	3. D	3. C	3. A
4. A	4. B	4. B	4. C	4. B	4. D
5. B	5. C	5. B			5. A
6. C		6. D			6. C
7. D		7. D			7. A
8. C					8. D
9. A					9. D

Chapter 18	Chapter 19
1. C	1. D
2. A	2. A
3. D	3. B
4. B	4. C
5. C	5. C
6. D	6. B
7. B	7. A
8. D	
9. C	
10. C	

PRE-READING VOCABULARY WORKSHEETS

VOCABULARY - *The Hobbit*

Chapter 1 Part I: Using Prior Knowledge and Contextual Clues

Below are the sentences in which the vocabulary words appear in the text. Read the sentence. Use any clues you can find in the sentence combined with your prior knowledge, and write what you think the underlined words mean in the space provided.

1. He liked visitors, but he liked to know them before they arrived, and he **preferred** to ask them himself.

2. . . . while the four dwarves sat around the table, and talked about mines and gold and troubles with the goblins, and the **depredations** of dragons, and lots of other things which he did not understand

3. "Put on a few gees, there's a good fellow!' Gandalf called after him, as the hobbit stumped off to the pantries. "And just bring out the cold chicken and pickles!"
"Seems to know as much about the inside of my **larders** as I do myself!" thought Mr. Baggins. . . .

4. Then Gandalf's smoke ring would go green and come back to hover over the wizard's head. He had quite a cloud of them about him already, and in the dim light it made him look strange and **sorcerous**.

5,6. We are not together in the house of our friend and fellow **conspirator**, this most excellent and **audacious** hobbit–may the hair on his toes never fall out! all praise to his wine and ale!

7. "Five feet high the door and three may walk abreast" say the **runes**, but Smaug could not creep into a hole that size, not even when he was a young dragon

8. Also I should like to know about the risks, out-of-pocket expenses, time required and **remuneration**, and so forth

Vocabulary - *The Hobbit* Chapter 1 Continued

Part II: Determining the Meaning   Match the vocabulary words to their dictionary definitions.

___ 1. prefer   A. daring; bold
___ 2. depredations   B. in command of magic, spells & witchcraft
___ 3. larders   C. payment
___ 4. sorcerous   D. to like better; rather
___ 5. conspirator   E. pantry or cupboards containing food stores
___ 6. audacious   F. one who joins in planning or plotting
___ 7. runes   G. words written in ancient Germanic letters
___ 8. remuneration   H. acts of preying upon others

Vocabulary - *The Hobbit* Chapters 2-3

Part I: Using Prior Knowledge and Contextual Clues
   Below are the sentences in which the vocabulary words appear in the text. Read the sentence. Use any clues you can find in the sentence combined with your prior knowledge, and write what you think the underlined words mean in the space provided.

1, 2. Thinking it unnecessary to disturb your esteemed **repose**, we have proceeded in advance to make **requisite** preparations, and shall await your respected person at the Green Dragon Inn

3. but there was a good deal of food jumbled carelessly on shelves and on the ground, among an untidy litter of **plunder**, of all sorts from brass buttons to pots full of gold coins standing in a corner.

4. These are not troll-make. They are old swords, very old swords of the High Elves of the West, my **kin**.

Part II: Determining the Meaning -- Match the vocabulary words to their dictionary definitions.

___ 1. repose   A. stolen property
___ 2. requisite   B. required; necessary
___ 3. plunder   C. relatives
___ 4. kin   D. rest

Vocabulary - *The Hobbit* Chapters 4-5

Part I: Using Prior Knowledge and Contextual Clues
    Below are the sentences in which the vocabulary words appear in the text. Read the sentence. Use any clues you can find in the sentence combined with your prior knowledge, and write what you think the underlined words mean in the space provided.

1. The nights were comfortless and chill, and they did not dare to sing or talk too loud, for the echoes were **uncanny**, and the silence seemed to dislike being broken

2. He know, of course, that the riddle game was sacred and of immense **antiquity**, and even wicked creatures were afraid to cheat when they played at it.

3. Gollum was in his boat again, paddling wildly back to the dark shore; and such a rage of loss and **suspicion** was in his heart that no sword had any more terror for him.

Part II: Determining the Meaning -- Match the vocabulary words to their dictionary definitions.

___ 1. uncanny   A. quality of being very old or ancient
___ 2. antiquity   B. unexplainable & strange, exciting wonder & fear
___ 3. suspicion   C. thinking something exists, especially something wrong, without any proof

Vocabulary - *The Hobbit* Chapter 6

Part I: Using Prior Knowledge and Contextual Clues

    Below are the sentences in which the vocabulary words appear in the text. Read the sentence. Use any clues you can find in the sentence combined with your prior knowledge, and write what you think the underlined words mean in the space provided.

1. He was on a stony path winding downwards with a rocky wall on the left hand; on the other side the ground sloped away and there were **dells** below the level of the path overhung with bushes and low trees.

2. If we have got to go back now into those **abominable** tunnels to look for him, then drat him, I say.

3. Then they shouted with surprise and delight. Gandalf was as **astonished** as any of them, but probably more pleased than all the others.

4. He loosed Dori's ankles with a gasp and fell onto the rough platform of an eagle's **eyrie**.

Part II: Determining the Meaning Match the vocabulary words to their dictionary definitions.

___ 1. dells   A. nest built on a high place
___ 2. abominable   B. small, secluded, wooded valley
___ 3. astonished   C. thoroughly unpleasant
___ 4. eyrie   D. surprised

Vocabulary - *The Hobbit* Chapter 7

Part I: Using Prior Knowledge and Contextual Clues
   Below are the sentences in which the vocabulary words appear in the text. Read the sentence. Use any clues you can find in the sentence combined with your prior knowledge, and write what you think the underlined words mean in the space provided.

1. The morning was cool, and mists were in the valleys and hollows and twined here and there about the peaks and **pinnacles** of the hills.

2. He was clothed in a **tunic** of wool down to his knees

3. That is Mr. Baggins, a hobbit of good family and **unimpeachable** reputation

4. It was difficult to think of **pursuing** goblins behind, and when they had put many miles between them and Beorn's house they began to talk and to sing again

5. Cheer up Thorin and Company! This is your **expedition** after all. Think of the treasure at the end, and forget the forest and the dragon

6. "Do we really have to go through?" groaned the hobbit.
   "Yes, you do!" said the wizard, "if you want to get to the other side. You must either go through or give up your **quest**. And I am not going to let you back out now, Mr. Baggins.

Part II: Determining the Meaning   Match the vocabulary words to their dictionary definitions.

   ___ 1. pinnacle   A. chasing
   ___ 2. tunic   B. top; high point
   ___ 3. unimpeachable   C. search
   ___ 4. pursuing   D. beyond doubt; unquestionable
   ___ 5. expedition   E. long, loose-fitting shirt or coat
   ___ 6. quest   F. a journey undertaken with a definite objective

Vocabulary - *The Hobbit* Chapter 8

Part I: Using Prior Knowledge and Contextual Clues

Below are the sentences in which the vocabulary words appear in the text. Read the sentence. Use any clues you can find in the sentence combined with your prior knowledge, and write what you think the underlined words mean.

1. As soon as they had landed he had bent his bow and fitted an arrow in case any hidden **guardian** of the boat appeared.

2. Suddenly on the path ahead appeared some white deer, a hind and fawns as snowy white as the **hart** had been dark.

3. There was nothing now to be done but to tighten the belts round their empty stomachs, and **hoist** their empty sacks and packs, and trudge along the track

4. . . . there were spiders huge and horrible sitting in the branches above him . . . . then in the silence and stillness of the wood he realised that these **loathsome** creatures were speaking one to another.

5. The idea came to him to . . . make them curious, excited and angry all at once . . . dancing among the trees he began to sing a song to **infuriate** them and bring them all after him

Part II: Determining the Meaning   Match the vocabulary words to their dictionary definitions.

___ 1. guardian   A. male deer
___ 2. hart   B. to make angry; enrage
___ 3. hoist   C. repulsive; disgusting
___ 4. loathsome   D. one who guards, protects, or defends
___ 5. infuriate   E. lift up

Vocabulary - *The Hobbit* Chapters 9-10

Part I: Using Prior Knowledge and Contextual Clues

Below are the sentences in which the vocabulary words appear in the text. Read the sentence. Use any clues you can find in the sentence combined with your prior knowledge, and write what you think the underlined words mean.

1. For Thorin had taken heart again hearing how the hobbit had rescued his companions from the spiders, and was determined once more not to **ransom** himself with promises to the king of a share in the treasure, until all hope of escaping in any other way had disappeared

2. They all thought their won shares in the treasure (which they quite regarded as theirs, in spite of their **plight** and the still unconquered dragon) would suffer seriously if the Wood-elves claimed part of it

3. The luck turned all right before long: the **eddying** current carried several barrels close ashore

4. . . . and there was a merry racket down by the river. . . . He . . . managed just in time to get on to the mass of casks without being noticed in the general **bustle**.

5. The rotting piles of a greater town could still be seen along the shores when the waters sank in a **drought**.

6. But lock nor bar may **hinder** the homecoming spoken of old.

7. The Elvenking was very powerful in those parts and the Master wished for no **enmity** with him

8. People were shouting inside the hall and outside it. The **quays** were thronged with hurrying feet.

Vocabulary - *The Hobbit* Chapter 9-10 Continued

Part II: Determining the Meaning   Match the vocabulary words to their dictionary definitions.

___ 1. ransom   A. situation of difficulty
___ 2. plight   B. delay; get in the way of
___ 3. eddying   C. release, give up, or free in return for payment
___ 4. bustle   D. going against the main current, especially in a swirling motion
___ 5. drought   E. wharf or reinforced bank where ships are loaded
___ 6. hinder   F. long period of time with no rain
___ 7. enmity   G. commotion, hurried activity
___ 8. quay   H. deep hatred

Vocabulary - *The Hobbit* Chapters 11-12

Part I: Using Prior Knowledge and Contextual Clues

Below are the sentences in which the vocabulary words appear in the text. Read the sentence. Use any clues you can find in the sentence combined with your prior knowledge, and write what you think the underlined words mean.

1. They were come to the Desolation of the Dragon, and they were come at the **waning** of the year.

2. . . . though autumn was now crawling towards winter that pleasant time now seemed years ago. They were alone in the **perilous** waste without hope of further help.

3. On this western side there were fewer signs of the dragon's **marauding** feet, and there was some grass for their ponies.

4. They beat on it, they thrust and pushed at it, they **implored** it to move, they spoke fragments of broken spells of opening, and nothing stirred.

5. When morning came the terror of the dwarves grew less. They realized that dangers of this kind were **inevitable** in dealing with such a guardian, and that it was no good giving up their quest yet.

6. Whenever Smaug's roving eye, seeking for him in the shadows, flashed across him, he trembled, and an unaccountable desire **seized** hold of him to rush out and reveal himself and tell all the truth to Smaug. In fact he was in grievous danger of coming under the dragon-spell.

7. And Smaug laughed aloud. He had a wicked and a **wily** heart, and he knew his guesses were not far out

8. Truly there can nowhere be found the equal of Lord Smaug the **Impenetrable**. What magnificence to possess a waistcoat of fine diamonds!

Vocabulary - *The Hobbit* Chapter 9-10 Continued

9. . . . they all began discussing dragon-slayings historical, **dubious**, and mythical, and the . . . devices and stratagems by which they had been accomplished.

10. —because at first he wanted to try and **lure** me in again, I suppose, and now perhaps because he is waiting till after tonight's hunt

Part II: Determining the Meaning   Match the vocabulary words to their dictionary definitions.

___ 1. waning   A. grabbed
___ 2. perilous   B. calculating; plotting
___ 3. marauding   C. entice; attract
___ 4. implored   D. lessening; going away; ending
___ 5. inevitable   E. wandering in search of something to steal
___ 6. seized   F. can't be pierced or entered through
___ 7. wily   G. dangerous
___ 8. impenetrable   H. ask or beg urgently
___ 9. dubious   I. unavoidable; going to happen no matter what
___ 10. lure   J. doubtful

Vocabulary - *The Hobbit* Chapters 13-15

Part I: Using Prior Knowledge and Contextual Clues

Below are the sentences in which the vocabulary words appear in the text. Read the sentence. Use any clues you can find in the sentence combined with your prior knowledge, and write what you think the underlined words mean.

1. A light helm of figured leather, strengthened beneath with hoops of steel, and studded about the rim with white gems, was set upon the hobbit's head. "I feel magnificent," he thought; "but I expect I look rather **absurd**. How they would laugh on the Hill at home! Still I wish there was a looking-glass handy!"

2. Mr. Baggins kept his head more clear of the bewitchment of the **hoard** than the dwarves did. Long before the dwarves were tired of examining the treasures, he became wary of it and sat down on the floor

3. In all their talk they came **perpetually** back to one thing: where was Smaug?

4. Probably most of them would have **perished** in the winter that now hurried after autumn, if help had not been to hand. But help came swiftly

5. The treasure was not his that his evil deeds should be **amended** with a share of it.

Part II: Determining the Meaning   Match the vocabulary words to their dictionary definitions.

___ 1. absurd   A. corrected; made better
___ 2. hoard   B. ridiculous
___ 3. perpetually   C. a gathered, hidden, or stored supply or treasure
___ 4. perish   D. continuously; always
___ 5. amended   E. die; pass from existence

Vocabulary - *The Hobbit* Chapters 16-19

Part I: Using Prior Knowledge and Contextual Clues

Below are the sentences in which the vocabulary words appear in the text. Read the sentence. Use any clues you can find in the sentence combined with your prior knowledge, and write what you think the underlined words mean.

1. But I have an interest in the matter–one fourteenth share, to be **precise**, according to a letter, which fortunately I believe I have kept.

2. Did you come to ask me idle questions? Still the elf-host has not departed as I bade! Till then you come in **vain** to bargain with me.

3. The Eagles had long had suspicion of the goblins' **mustering**: from their watchfulness the movements in the mountains could not be altogether hid.

4. Yet a fourteenth share of all the silver and gold, **wrought** and unwrought, was given up to Bard

5. One autumn evening some years afterwards Bilbo was sitting in his study writing his **memoirs**– he thought of calling them "There and Back Again, a Hobbit's Holiday"–when there was a ring at the door.

Part II: Determining the Meaning   Match the vocabulary words to their dictionary definitions.

___ 1. precise   A. lacking substance; hollow; fruitless
___ 2. vain   B. gathering
___ 3. mustering   C. narrative of experiences an author has lived through
___ 4. wrought   D. shaped; worked
___ 5. memoirs   E. exact

ANSWER KEY - VOCABULARY
The Hobbit

Chapter 1	Chapters 2-3	Chapters 4-5	Chapter 6	Chapter 7	Chapter 8
1. D	1. D	1. B	1. B	1. B	1. D
2. H	2. B	2. A	2. C	2. E	2. A
3. E	3. A	3. C	3. D	3. D	3. E
4. B	4. C		4. A	4. A	4. C
5. F				5. F	5. B
6. A				6. C	
7. G					
8. C					

Chapters 9-10	Chapters 11-12	Chapters 13-15	Chapters 16-19
1. C	1. D	1. B	1. E
2. A	2. G	2. C	2. A
3. D	3. E	3. D	3. B
4. G	4. H	4. E	4. D
5. F	5. I	5. A	5. C
6. B	6. A		
7. H	7. B		
8. E	8. F		
	9. J		
	10. C		

DAILY LESSONS

LESSON ONE

Objectives
1. To introduce students to *The Hobbit* as an adventure story
2. To get students thinking about adventures they have had or would like to have, to help them apply the idea of "adventure" to their own lives
3. To give students the opportunity to practice their creative writing skills

Activity #1

Distribute Writing Assignment #1 and discuss the directions in detail. Give students the remainder of this class period to work on this assignment. While students are working on this assignment, distribute/assign the books to students. (If you wish, you may also distribute the other materials which students will need for the unit. There is, however, time planned for distributing materials in Lesson Two. If your students tend to lose materials or tend to forget to bring what they need to class, you might wait to give the materials out in Lesson Two when you will also need students' attention to tell them how these materials are to be used.)

Determine the amount of time your students will need to complete this assignment to your standards, and tell them when the paper will be due. Tell students exactly what you expect regarding length of the story and the elements on which they will be graded. This can be a simple composition of a page or two, simply to introduce the idea of an adventure story, or it can be as elaborate and demanding as you think your students can handle.

Give students the remainder of this class period to begin working on this writing assignment.

WRITING ASSIGNMENT #1 - *The Hobbit*

PROMPT

The Hobbit, the book you are about to read, is, among other things, a story of adventure. That is, a story that tells about the adventures of a character or a group of characters. Adventure stories can be true or fiction; they can be about things that really happened to someone, or they can be completely made-up. The story of *The Hobbit* is completely made up, about goblins, elves, dwarves, a wizard, and, of course, the hobbit.

Your assignment is to write an adventure story in which you are the main character. You can base your story on some events that have actually happened to you, or you can completely make up everything in your story. Remember, your story needs to start somewhere, continue through a series of events or adventures, and come to a close at the end of the adventures.

PRE-WRITING

Think of an adventure you might have had. It could be a vacation your family has taken, a single day that was extraordinary in some way (maybe exceptionally good or exceptionally bad), or maybe even a dream you've had in which you had an adventure. Or, you could think of an adventure you would LIKE to have (or maybe would *dread* having!) In your mind's eye picture the events that took place (or would take place). Jot down a few words about each main event on the adventure, and put them in chronological order (in the time-order they happen).

DRAFTING

There are innumerable ways to begin writing your story. The important thing is to get your reader into the setting; the reader needs to understand the place, time, mood, what is going on, and who is involved. Think of ways some books you have read have started. Some start right in the middle of the action. Some start with a description of the setting. Some start with dialogue. Choose your opening, and begin writing, following the notes you made in the pre-writing step above. In the drafting stage, the point is to get your ideas down on paper, from start to finish.

REVISING

After you have finished a rough draft of your composition, revise it yourself until you are happy with your work. Be sure to include action verbs and descriptive words (adjectives) to make your story come to life for your reader. Don't get stuck in the "and then this happened, and then that happened" rut. Make an effort to really make your story pop off of the page for your reader. If you need to write dialogue, look in another book you have read to see how to punctuate and write it. Go back and reread your story several times, making corrections until you think it's perfect. Then, ask a student who sits near you to read it and tell you what he/she likes best about your work, and what things he/she thinks can be improved. Take another look at your story keeping in mind your critic's suggestions, and make the revisions you feel are necessary.

LESSON TWO

Objectives
1. To distribute and discuss materials students will use in this unit
2. To preview and begin reading *The Hobbit*
3. To evaluate students' oral reading

Activity #1

Distribute the materials students will use in this unit. Explain in detail how students are to use these materials.

Study Guides Students should preview the study guide questions before each reading assignment to get a feeling for what events and ideas are important in that section. After reading the section, students will (as a class or individually) answer the questions to review the important events and ideas from that section of the book. Students should keep the study guides as study materials for the unit test.

Vocabulary Prior to reading a reading assignment, students will do vocabulary work related to the section of the book they are about to read. Following the completion of the reading of the book, there will be a vocabulary review of all the words used in the vocabulary assignments. Students should keep their vocabulary work as study materials for the unit test.

Reading Assignment Sheet You need to fill in the reading assignment sheet to let students know when their reading has to be completed. You can either write the assignment sheet on a side blackboard or bulletin board and leave it there for students to see each day, or you can make copies for each student to have. In either case, you should advise students to become very familiar with the reading assignments so they know what is expected of them.

Extra Activities Center The Unit Resource Materials portion of this unit contains suggestions for a library of related books and articles in your classroom as well as puzzles and other worksheets. Make an extra activities center in your room where you will keep these materials for students to use. (Bring the books and articles in from the library and keep several copies of the puzzles and worksheets on hand.) Explain to students that these materials are available for students to use when they finish reading assignments or other class work early.

Nonfiction Assignment Sheet Explain to students that they each are to read at least one non-fiction piece from the in-class library at some time during the unit. Students will fill out a nonfiction assignment sheet after completing the reading to help you evaluate their reading experiences and to help the students think about and evaluate their own reading experiences.

<u>Books</u> Each school has its own rules and regulations regarding student use of school books. Advise students of the procedures that are normal for your school.

<u>Activity #2</u>

Briefly review the study questions for chapter 1 of *The Hobbit*. Explain to students that they should read the study questions for each assignment prior to reading that assignment.

<u>Activity #3</u>

Do the vocabulary worksheet for chapter 1 of *The Hobbit* together, orally, in class so students can see how it works. Explain that they will be expected to do a vocabulary worksheet prior to each reading assignment.

<u>Activity#4</u>

Have students read chapter 1 of *The Hobbit* out loud in class. You probably know the best way to get readers within your class; pick students at random, ask for volunteers, or use whatever method works best for your group. If you have not yet completed an oral reading evaluation for your students this marking period, this would be a good opportunity to do so. A form is included with this unit for your convenience.

If students do not complete reading chapter 1 in class, they should do so prior to your next class meeting.

NONFICTION ASSIGNMENT SHEET - *The Hobbit*
(To be completed after reading the required nonfiction article)

Name _____ Date _____

Title of Nonfiction Read _____

Written By _____ Publication Date _____

I. Factual Summary: Write a short summary of the piece you read.

II. Vocabulary
    1. With which vocabulary words in the piece did you encounter some degree of difficulty?

    2. How did you resolve your lack of understanding with these words?

III. Interpretation: What was the main point the author wanted you to get from reading his work?

IV. Criticism
    1. With which points of the piece did you agree or find easy to accept? Why?

    2. With which points of the piece did you disagree or find difficult to believe? Why?

V. Personal Response: What do you think about this piece? <u>OR</u> How does this piece influence your ideas?

ORAL READING EVALUATION - *The Hobbit*

Name _____ Class____ Date _____

SKILL	EXCELLENT	GOOD	AVERAGE	FAIR	POOR
Fluency	5	4	3	2	1
Clarity	5	4	3	2	1
Audibility	5	4	3	2	1
Pronunciation	5	4	3	2	1
_____	5	4	3	2	1
_____	5	4	3	2	1

Total _____   Grade _____

Comments:

LESSON THREE

Objectives
    1. To review the main ideas and events of chapter 1
    2. To preview the study questions and vocabulary for chapters 2-3
    3. To read chapters 2-3
    4. To continue and complete the oral reading evaluations

Activity #1

    Discuss the answers to the study questions for chapter 1 in detail. Write the answers on the board or overhead transparency so students can have the correct answers for study purposes. Note: It is a good practice in public speaking and leadership skills for individual students to take charge of leading the discussions of the study questions. Perhaps a different student could go to the front of the class and lead the discussion each day that the study questions are discussed during this unit. Of course, the teacher should guide the discussion when appropriate and be sure to fill in any gaps the students leave.

Activity #2

    Give students about fifteen minutes to preview the study questions for chapters 2-3 of *The Hobbit* and to do the related vocabulary work.

Activity #3

    Continue your oral reading evaluations as students read chapters 2-3 of *The Hobbit* orally in class. If students do not complete reading chapters 2-3 in class, they should do so prior to the next class meeting.

LESSON FOUR

Objectives
1. To give students the opportunity to practice persuasive writing
2. To get students to think about Bilbo and the pros and cons of his quest
3. To preview the study questions and vocabulary for chapters 4-5

Activity #1

Distribute Writing Assignment #2 and discuss the directions in detail. Allow the remaining class time for students to complete the assignment. Collect the papers at the end of the class period.

Follow - Up: After you have graded the assignments, have a writing conference with the students. (This unit schedules one in Lesson Eight.) After the writing conference, allow students to revise their papers using your suggestions and corrections. Give them about three days from the date they receive their papers to complete the revision. I suggest grading the revisions on an A-C-E scale (all revisions well-done, some revisions made, few or no revisions made). This will speed your grading time and still give some credit for the students' efforts.

Activity #2

Tell students that if they finish the reading assignment early, they should preview the study questions and do the pre-reading vocabulary work for chapters 4-5. This assignment should be completed by all students prior to the next class period.

WRITING ASSIGNMENT #2 - *The Hobbit*

PROMPT
You now know a little bit about Bilbo, the dwarves, Gandalf, and that they are going to try to return to the mountain to destroy the dragon and reclaim Thorin's lands and treasures. Unsuspecting Bilbo has been chosen to help Thorin and Company on this quest. Your assignment is to decide whether or not you think going on this quest is a good idea for Bilbo and to either persuade him to go or NOT to go.

PRE-WRITING
First, you need to decide if you think Bilbo should go or not. Make a list of the benefits of going, then make a list of the negative aspects of the trip. Decide whether you want to persuade Bilbo to go or NOT to go. Write your composition as if you were talking to Bilbo as his friend. Jot down a few notes about how you would bring up the subject. Make a list of reasons why you think he should/should not go (based on your list of benefits and negative aspects of the trip). Jot down a few notes about how you would end the conversation– your parting words.

DRAFTING
Using your notes from the pre-writing section above, write out exactly what you would say to Bilbo. Begin with an introductory paragraph in which you bring up the subject and state your point. Continue with a paragraph for each of the main reasons you wrote down, giving further details, explanations, or examples to support each reason. End with a concluding paragraph which would end the conversation.

REVISING
When you finish the rough draft of your paper, read over it again. Does it make sense? Did you leave out any words or ideas? Could any points be presented better? When you are satisfied with your work, ask a student who sits near you to read it. After reading your rough draft, he/she should tell you what he/she liked best about your work, which parts were difficult to understand, and ways in which your work could be improved. Reread your paper considering your critic's comments, and make the corrections you think are necessary.

PROOFREADING
Do a final proofreading of your paper double-checking your grammar, spelling, organization, and the clarity of your ideas.

LESSON FIVE

Objectives
   1. To review the main events and ideas of chapters 2-3
   2. To read chapters 4-5

Activity #1
   Discuss the study questions for chapters 2-3. You could use the multiple choice questions as a quiz to make sure students did the required reading and then discuss the answers, or you could simply use the short answer study questions as a guide to discussing the main events in these chapters.

Activity #2
   Give students the remainder of this class period to read chapters 4-5. If you have not completed the oral reading evaluations, you could have students read orally and complete the evaluations in this session. If you have completed the oral reading assignments, you could let students read silently.

LESSON SIX

Objectives
   1. To review the main events and ideas from chapters 4-5
   2. To preview and read chapter 6

Activity #1
   Discuss the study questions for chapters 4-5. You could use the multiple choice questions as a quiz to make sure students did the required reading and then discuss the answers, or you could simply use the short answer study questions as a guide to discussing the main events in these chapters.

Activity #2
   Give students about 15 minutes to preview the study questions and do the vocabulary worksheet for chapter 6. This could be done individually or in small groups.

Activity #3
   Give students the remainder of this class period to read chapter 6. They could read orally or silently–or you could pair students up in small groups of 1-4 students and have each take a turn reading orally to the others in the group, alternating paragraphs.

LESSON SEVEN

Objectives
1. To review the main ideas and events from chapter 6
2. To preview and read chapter 7
3. To hold writing conferences with individual students

Activity #1

Discuss the study questions for chapter 6. You could use the multiple choice questions as a quiz to make sure students did the required reading and then discuss the answers, or you could simply use the short answer study questions as a guide to discussing the main events in these chapters.

Activity #2

Give students about 15 minutes to preview the study questions and do the vocabulary worksheet for chapter 7. This could be done individually or in small groups.

Activity #3

Give students the remainder of this class period to silently read chapter 7.

Activity #4

While students are doing the pre-reading and reading work for chapter 7, call individual students to a private area in your room to discuss their writing, using Writing Assignment #2 as a basis for the conference. Make suggestions as to how their work could have been improved, and tell them to write a revision of Writing Assignment #2 based on your comments. Tell each student when the revision should be turned in for grading.

WRITING EVALUATION FORM - *The Hobbit*

Name _____ Date _____

Writing Assignment #2 for the *The Hobbit* unit Grade _____

Grammar:	excellent	good	fair	poor (errors noted)
Spelling:	excellent	good	fair	poor (errors noted)
Punctuation:	excellent	good	fair	poor (errors noted)
Legibility:	excellent	good	fair	poor
Persuasiveness:	excellent	good	fair	poor

Strengths:

Weaknesses:

Comments/Suggestions:

LESSONS EIGHT AND NINE

Objectives
    1. To discuss the main ideas and events for chapter 7 of *The Hobbit*
    2. To introduce the project for this unit
    3. To assign the pre-reading and reading work for chapter 8

Activity #1
    Discuss the study questions for chapter 7. You could use the multiple choice questions as a quiz to make sure students did the required reading and then discuss the answers, or you could simply use the short answer study questions as a guide to discussing the main events in these chapters.

Activity #2
    Explain the project to students and give them this class period and the next one (Lessons Eight and Nine) to work on the project in class.

Activity #3
    Tell students that prior to Lesson 10 they should preview the study questions, do the vocabulary worksheet and do the reading for chapter 8.

THE HOBBIT PROJECT
(Teacher)

OBJECTIVE
There are so many things to delve into in this book that unless you spend a whole term (or longer) on it, you'll only have time to scratch the surface. The purpose of this project is to divide and conquer the workload of going into at least a little depth about several different topics associated with the book.

THE PROJECT
Below is a list of *some* topics in the book your students could explore further. It is in no way a complete list of possible topics. If you are a Tolkien fan and are really into his world, there are *many* other topics you could add to this list. This list is just intended as a suggested starting point to cover some of the basic elements in the story.

The project is to assign one topic to each student or one topic to a small group (2-3) of students. The students then should look in the text for all references to their topic, check alternate sources for information about that topic, prepare to give a report and lead a discussion about their topic, and submit a written report (Writing Assignment #3).

SOME TOPICS

The Lands	Bilbo
The Songs and Riddles	Gandalf
Food/Eating	Thorin
Bravery/Courage	Beorn
Morality/Conscience–Right Versus Wrong	Gollum
Appearance Versus Reality	Smaug
Weather Related To Events	The Dwarves
Light and Dark Imagery	The Trolls
Folklore/ History	The Goblins
Water	The Elves
Magic	The Eagles
Names of Places	The Wargs
Senses	Men
Motives	The Ring
Swords/Knives/Wand/Weaponry	Signs And Symbols

THE HOBBIT PROJECT INSTRUCTIONS
(Student)

TOPIC
The topic you have been assigned for this project is _____.

THE PROJECT
Your assignment is to :

1. Look in the book *The Hobbit* for all references to your topic. Make notes about the page number on which the references appear and briefly what relevant information is on each page. Take a few sheets of notebook paper and make three columns–a small one for the page number, a bigger one where you can jot down notes about the information on the page, and a third one where you can make notes about the importance of the reference you have found. You should make bold horizontal lines to separate chapters for easy reference. You can begin doing this part now, going back over the chapters you have already read, and continue your reference chart as you continue reading the rest of the book. If you have a huge topic, like Bilbo, for example, you should choose references that are the most meaningful, not just *every* reference to him in the book.

2. Check alternate sources for more information about your topic, and make notes from these sources. The Internet has *lots* of information about *The Hobbit*, and there are many books and articles written about this book, its characters, and the world created by Tolkien. Be sure to keep a bibliography, a list of all the sources you use.

3. Prepare to give an oral report about your topic to the class. You should make a presentation to the class about your topic. The presentation should last 3 to 5 minutes and should relate to the class the most important and interesting things you found relating to your topic. You may use visual aids to help make your points clear to the class. You may use an outline to keep your oral presentation on track. Be prepared to answer questions your classmates may have about your presentation or your topic.

4. Write a report about your topic. This will include more detailed information than your oral report. In this written report, you should thoroughly but succinctly explain all that your research and thought about your topic produced. Writing Assignment #3 will guide you through the writing of this report.

DUE DATES

Your Oral Report Will Be Given On _____.

Your Written Report Will Be Turned In On _____.

WRITING ASSIGNMENT #3 - *The Hobbit*

PROMPT
You have a lot of information about your assigned project topic, and you need to turn it into a written report.

PRE-WRITING
Much of your pre-writing work has already been done. You should have pages with text references, notes about what you found in the book, and notes you have taken from alternate sources.

Reread your notes. Jot down categories of information you have collected. Under each category, put the basic facts you have collected. If you took your notes on index cards, organizing your ideas will be pretty easy; just put them in one pile for each category.

Consider the categories of information you have--everything you have discovered through your research. If you had to make one general statement that covered everything important about your topic, what would it be? That, then will be the main point of your paper.

DRAFTING
You'll introduce your main point in an introductory paragraph. Follow that with one paragraph for each relevant category of information, using a topic sentence to state the main point of the category and then using your facts as supporting details within each paragraph. End your paper with a concluding paragraph.

REVISING
Read through what you have written. Does it make sense? Do your ideas flow smoothly and logically? Was everything you included relevant to your topic? Make any revisions you think are necessary.

PROOFREADING
When you are satisfied with your work, give it to a fellow student or a parent to read. Ask that person to tell you anything that needs to be explained better or presented more clearly. Consider the suggestions made to you, and revise your paper as you deem necessary. Be sure to double check your mechanics (spelling, punctuation, capitalization, etc.).

LESSON TEN

Objectives
1. To review the main events and ideas from chapter 8
2. To preview and read chapters 9-10

Activity #1
Discuss the study questions for chapter 8. You could use the multiple choice questions as a quiz to make sure students did the required reading and then discuss the answers, or you could simply use the short answer study questions as a guide to discussing the main events in these chapters.

Activity #2
Give students about 15 minutes to preview the study questions and do the vocabulary worksheet for chapters 9-10. This could be done individually or in small groups.

Activity #3
Give students the remainder of this class period to silently read chapters 9-10.

LESSON ELEVEN

Objectives
1. To review the main ideas and events from chapters 9-10
2. To preview and read chapters 11-12
3. To give students time to work on their projects

Activity #1
Discuss the study questions for chapters 9-10. You could use the multiple choice questions as a quiz to make sure students did the required reading and then discuss the answers, or you could simply use the short answer study questions as a guide to discussing the main events in these chapters.

Activity #2
Tell students that prior to the next class period, they need to have done the pre-reading and reading work for chapters 11-12. Give them the option of doing this assignment now and working on their projects for homework or working on their projects now and doing the reading assignments for homework.

LESSON TWELVE

Objectives
1. To review the main ideas and events from chapters 11-12
2. To give students the opportunity to work on their nonfiction assignments
3. To do the pre-reading and reading work for chapters 13-15

NOTE: Meet this class period in the school library or media center where students will have reference resources readily available.

Activity #1

Discuss the study questions for chapters 11-12. You could use the multiple choice questions as a quiz to make sure students did the required reading and then discuss the answers, or you could simply use the short answer study questions as a guide to discussing the main events in these chapters.

Activity #2

Remind students that they have to complete a nonfiction reading assignment for this unit; they have to read an article or book about some non-fiction topic related to *The Hobbit* and complete the nonfiction assignment sheet. Here is a list of some suggested topics:

Modern Treasure Hunting	Lands Beyond–Places To Visit And What To See There
Careers in Archeology	
Travel Tips	All About Eagles
Reports of Ghosts, Goblins & Haunted Houses	Modern Magicians
Medical Research About Genes or Diseases That Cause Dwarfism in Humans	War, Warfare, or Specific Battles
	Archery
Ancient Weapons and Armor	Precious Stones/Noteworthy Gems
The Life And Writings of J. R. R. Tolkien	Careers in the Military or as a Private Guard
Differences in Food/Eating Habits In Various Cultures	The History of Rings
	Tea–Kinds, Uses, History
Modern Day Heroes	All About Spiders
Music and Music Lyrics, Modern or Historical	

Activity #4

Tell students that prior to the next class period they need to do the pre-reading work and read chapters 13-15.

LESSON THIRTEEN

Objectives
1. To review the main ideas and events from chapters 13-15
2. To have students share the nonfiction information they gathered
3. To do the pre-reading and reading work for chapters 16-19

Activity #1

Discuss the study questions for chapters 13-15. You could use the multiple choice questions as a quiz to make sure students did the required reading and then discuss the answers, or you could simply use the short answer study questions as a guide to discussing the main events in these chapters.

Activity #2

Have students give a brief, oral summary of the nonfiction piece they read. You could do this calling on individual students, so the whole class hears about all the articles, or you could have students get in groups of 4, tell about their articles to each other, then have them regroup with others with whom they have not been previously grouped. Do this three or four times so all students are exposed to information about many different articles.

Activity #3

Review the study questions and do the vocabulary worksheet for chapters 16-19 together, orally, in class. Assign the reading of chapters 16-19 to be completed prior to your next class period. If students finish the oral work early, they may begin on the reading assignment for the remainder of the class period.

LESSON FOURTEEN

Objectives
1. To review the main events and ideas from chapters 16-19
2. To give students time to work on their written reports (Writing Assignment #3) in class so help is available

Activity #1
　　　Discuss the study questions for chapters 16-19. You could use the multiple choice questions as a quiz to make sure students did the required reading and then discuss the answers, or you could simply use the short answer study questions as a guide to discussing the main events in these chapters.

Activity #2
　　　Give students the remainder of this period to work on their written reports for the project. Walk around the room and check on the progress of each student, seeing if anyone is especially stuck or has questions. If many students are having a problem, you may want to take 5-10 minutes to give additional class instruction.

LESSON FIFTEEN

Objective
　　　To review all the vocabulary words studied in this unit

Activity
　　　Choose one (or more) of the vocabulary review activities listed on the next page(s) and spend your class period as directed in the activity. Some of the materials for these review activities are located in the Vocabulary Resource Materials section in this unit.

VOCABULARY REVIEW ACTIVITIES

1. Divide your class into two teams and have an old-fashioned spelling or definition bee.

2. Give each of your students (or students in groups of two, three or four) a *Of Mice and Men* Vocabulary Word Search Puzzle. The person (group) to find all of the vocabulary words in the puzzle first wins.

3. Give students a *The Hobbit* Vocabulary Word Search Puzzle without the word list. The person or group to find the most vocabulary words in the puzzle wins.

4. Use a *The Hobbit* Vocabulary Crossword Puzzle. Put the puzzle onto a transparency on the overhead projector (so everyone can see it), and do the puzzle together as a class.

5. Give students a *The Hobbit* Vocabulary Matching Worksheet to do.

6. Divide your class into two teams. Use *The Hobbit* vocabulary words with their letters jumbled as a word list. Student 1 from Team A faces off against Student 1 from Team B. You write the first jumbled word on the board. The first student (1A or 1B) to unscramble the word wins the chance for his/her team to score points. If 1A wins the jumble, go to student 2A and give him/her a definition. He/she must give you the correct spelling of the vocabulary word which fits that definition. If he/she does, Team A scores a point, and you give student 3A a definition for which you expect a correctly spelled matching vocabulary word. Continue giving Team A definitions until some team member makes an incorrect response. An incorrect response sends the game back to the jumbled-word face off, this time with students 2A and 2B. Instead of repeating giving definitions to the first few students of each team, continue with the student after the one who gave the last incorrect response on the team. For example, if Team B wins the jumbled-word face-off, and student 5B gave the last incorrect answer for Team B, you would start this round of definition questions with student 6B, and so on. The team with the most points wins!

LESSON SIXTEEN

Objectives
1. To discuss the ideas and themes from *The Hobbit* in greater detail
2. To have students exercise their critical thinking skills
3. To try to relate some of the ideas in *The Hobbit* to the students' lives

Activity #1

Choose the questions from the Extra Discussion Questions/Writing Assignments which seem most appropriate for your students. A class discussion of these questions is most effective if students have been given the opportunity to formulate answers to the questions prior to the discussion. To this end, you may either have all the students formulate answers to all the questions, divide your class into groups and assign one or more questions to each group, or you could assign one question to each student in your class. The option you choose will make a difference in the amount of class time needed for this activity.

Activity #2

After students have had ample time to formulate answers to the questions, begin your class discussion of the questions and the ideas presented by the questions. Be sure students take notes during the discussion so they have information to study for the unit test.

NOTE: The Extra Discussion Questions in this unit are somewhat abbreviated because much of the more in-depth material should be covered in the project presentations, in the lesson(s) following this one. If you have chosen not to use the project in this unit, you could take the topics listed there and easily formulate discussion questions from them.

EXTRA DISCUSSION QUESTIONS/WRITING ASSIGNMENTS
The Hobbit

Interpretive

1. From what point of view is the story told, and why is that important?

2. What is the setting, and what does it add to the story?

3. Are the characters in *The Hobbit* stereotypes? If so, give specific examples and explain the usefulness of employing stereotypes in the book. If they are not, explain how they merit individuality.

4. What are the main conflicts in the story, and how are they resolved?

5. What are three main themes presented in *The Hobbit*?

Critical

6. Explain the significance of the title "*The Hobbit*".

7. Compare and contrast Thorin and Bilbo.

8. What was Gandalf's purpose in the story?

9. List as "Good Guy" or "Bad Guy" and justify your answer: Gandalf, elves, eagles, Beorn, Thorin, Bilbo, trolls, Gollum, goblins, Smaug, Bard, Roäc, spiders, Dain, wargs.

10. Who is the main character in *The Hobbit*? Justify your answer.

11. Describe Tolkien's writing style. How does it influence our perception of the story?

Critical/Personal Response

12. Is the story of *The Hobbit* believable? Why or why not?

13. Is *The Hobbit* more than just an adventure story? Why or why not?

14. Choose another title for this book and justify your choice.

15. Which character in the book is the least honorable? Justify your answer.

16. What was the worst part of this quest for Bilbo? Why?

The Hobbit Extra Discussion Questions page 2

17. Choose two quotations from *The Hobbit* that are particularly important in the story and explain their importance.

18. What did Gandalf mean when, at the end of the book, he said to Bilbo, "You don't really suppose, do you, that all your adventures and escapes were managed by mere luck, just for your sole benefit? You are a very fine person, Mr. Baggins, and I am very fond of you; but you are only quite a little fellow in a wide world after all!"

Personal Response
19. Would you recommend this book to a friend? Why or why not?

20. Knowing what Thorin and Company had to go through and knowing how it all ended, would you have wanted to go on this quest?

21. Which character was your favorite? Why?

22. Given the opportunity, would you go on a modern day treasure hunt even though there would be great risks to you and NOT knowing whether or not you would find the treasure in the end?

LESSONS SEVENTEEN AND EIGHTEEN

Objectives
1. To expose all students to more depth about various aspects of *The Hobbit*
2. To give students the opportunity to practice public speaking
3. To discuss *The Hobbit*'s themes. symbols, ideas, and construction

Activity

Use this class period and the next (and an additional one, if it is needed) to have students give their oral presentations about their topics on *The Hobbit* and to hold additional discussions as necessary. If your students have done a reasonably good job with their research, these few days should be meaty discussion days regarding the book. It is well worth taking a little extra time during these presentations to follow up with questions, ideas and thoughts about the *many* intriguing aspects of this book.

LESSON NINETEEN

Objective

To review the main ideas presented in *The Hobbit*

Activity #1

Choose one of the review games/activities included in the packet and spend your class period as outlined there. Some materials for these activities are located in the Unit Resource section of this unit.

Activity #2

Remind students that the Unit Test will be in the next class meeting. Stress the review of the Study Guides and their class notes as a last minute, brush-up review for homework.

REVIEW GAMES/ACTIVITIES - *The Hobbit*

1. Ask the class to make up a unit test for *The Hobbit*. The test should have 4 sections: matching, true/false, short answer, and essay. Students may use 1/2 period to make the test and then swap papers and use the other 1/2 class period to take a test a classmate has devised. (open book) You may want to use the unit test included in this packet or take questions from the students' unit tests to formulate your own test.

2. Take 1/2 period for students to make up true and false questions (including the answers). Collect the papers and divide the class into two teams. Draw a big tic-tac-toe board on the chalk board. Make one team X and one team O. Ask questions to each side, giving each student one turn. If the question is answered correctly, that students' team's letter (X or O) is placed in the box. If the answer is incorrect, no mark is placed in the box. The object is to get three marks in a row like tic-tac-toe. You may want to keep track of the number of games won for each team.

3. Take 1/2 period for students to make up questions (true/false and short answer). Collect the questions. Divide the class into two teams. You'll alternate asking questions to individual members of teams A & B (like in a spelling bee). The question keeps going from A to B until it is correctly answered, then a new question is asked. A correct answer does not allow the team to get another question. Correct answers are +2 points; incorrect answers are -1 point.

4. Have students pair up and quiz each other from their study guides and class notes.

5. Give students a *The Hobbit* crossword puzzle to complete.

6. Divide your class into two teams. Use the *The Hobbit* crossword words with their letters jumbled as a word list. Student 1 from Team A faces off against Student 1 from Team B. You write the first jumbled word on the board. The first student (1A or 1B) to unscramble the word wins the chance for his/her team to score points. If 1A wins the jumble, go to student 2A and give him/her a clue. He/she must give you the correct word which matches that clue. If he/she does, Team A scores a point, and you give student 3A a clue for which you expect another correct response. Continue giving Team A clues until some team member makes an incorrect response. An incorrect response sends the game back to the jumbled-word face off, this time with students 2A and 2B. Instead of repeating giving clues to the first few students of each team, continue with the student after the one who gave the last incorrect response on the team. For example, if Team B wins the jumbled-word face-off, and student 5B gave the last incorrect answer for Team B, you would start this round of clue questions with student 6B, and so on.

UNIT TESTS

SHORT ANSWER UNIT TEST #1 - *The Hobbit*

I. Matching/Identify

___ 1. Gandalf
___ 2. Thorin
___ 3. Bilbo
___ 4. Dale
___ 5. Smaug
___ 6. Trolls
___ 7. Dwarves
___ 8. Elrond
___ 9. Orcrist
___ 10. Gollum
___ 11. Wargs
___ 12. Eagles
___ 13. Beorn
___ 14. Bard
___ 15. Roäc

A. William, Bert & Tom
B. killed the dragon
C. saved Thorin & Co. from goblins, wolves & fire
D. bear-man
E. King of the Elves
F. wizard
G. sword
H. small, slimy water creature
I. His grandfather was King of the Mountain
J. raven
K. Thorin, Dori, Bofur, & Ori, for example
L. hobbit
M. dragon
N. town ruins in the shadow of the mountain
O. wolves

II. Short Answer

1. Some of Bilbo's ancestors were Tooks. What influence did the Took genes have on Bilbo?

2. What did the dwarves think of Bilbo in the beginning of the adventure? What was the first event that started to change their minds about him? What did they think of him in the end of the story?

3. What was the point of this quest and was this goal achieved?

4. When did Bilbo first wish that he were back home?

The Hobbit Short Answer Test 1 page 2

5. What important information did Elrond give the travelers on their way to Misty Mountain?

6. How did Bilbo discover the power of the ring?

7. How did Gandalf get rid of the wargs and goblins? Did it work?

8. Beorn warned them about some things in Mirkwood. What?

9. When did Bilbo first realize he could be courageous and bold?

10. Why were the travelers actually glad to be captured by the wood elves?

11. What was the Arkenstone? Trace who held it throughout the story.

The Hobbit Short Answer Test 1 page 3

12. What started the whole argument/war between the dwarves and the townspeople, represented by Bard?

13. What did Bilbo miss at the end of the battle while he was knocked out?

14. What, besides spoons, did Bilbo lose?

15. What were Gandalf's last words to Bilbo in this book?

The Hobbit Short Answer Unit Test 1 page 4

III. Essay

Choose the single most important point you think Tolkien was making in *The Hobbit*. State that point, explain why you chose it, and explain how it is made through the events and characters in the book.

The Hobbit Short Answer Unit Test 1 page 5

IV. Vocabulary
   Listen to the vocabulary words and spell them.
   After you have spelled all the words, go back and write down the definitions.

   1.

   2.

   3.

   4.

   5.

   6.

   7.

   8.

   9.

   10.

ANSWER KEY SHORT ANSWER UNIT TEST #1 - *The Hobbit*

I. Matching/Identify

F	1. Gandalf	A. William, Bert & Tom
I	2. Thorin	B. killed the dragon
L	3. Bilbo	C. saved Thorin & Co. from goblins, wolves & fire
N	4. Dale	D. bear-man
M	5. Smaug	E. King of the Elves
A	6. Trolls	F. wizard
K	7. Dwarves	G. sword
E	8. Elrond	H. small, slimy water creature
G	9. Orcrist	I. His grandfather was King of the Mountain
H	10. Gollum	J. raven
O	11. Wargs	K. Thorin, Dori, Bofur, & Ori, for example
C	12. Eagles	L. hobbit
D	13. Beorn	M. dragon
B	14. Bard	N. town ruins in the shadow of the mountain
J	15. Roäc	O. wolves

II. Short Answer

1. Some of Bilbo's ancestors were Tooks. What influence did the Took genes have on Bilbo?
   They made him more adventurous than most other hobbits, which was a good thing related to this adventure.

2. What did the dwarves think of Bilbo in the beginning of the adventure? What was the first event that started to change their minds about him? What did they think of him in the end of the story?
   They thought he was a coward in the beginning. They started to change their minds when he told them of his adventure with Gollum. At the end of the book they respect his courage and heroic abilities.

3. What was the point of this quest and was this goal achieved?
   The point was to reclaim the lands and treasures of the dwarves from Smaug. Yes.

4. When did Bilbo first wish that he were back home?
   The travelers had passed through the hobbit lands and had gone into the Lone-lands where roads were bad, castles had an evil look, and the weather had turned cold and wet. He was tired and cold and wet.

The Hobbit Answer Key Short Answer Test 1 page 2

5. What important information did Elrond give the travelers on their way to Misty Mountain?
    He identified the swords Gandalf and Thorin had taken from the trolls' cave as being very old swords made by the High Elves of the West, his kin, for the Goblin-wars. Thorin's sword was named Orcrist, the Goblin-cleaver. Gandalf's was named Glamdring, the Foe-hammer, and was once worn by the King of Gondolin. He also read the moon-letters to reveal the way to open the secret door on the side of the mountain.

6. How did Bilbo discover the power of the ring?
    Gollum suspected Bilbo may have his ring, so he kept asking what Bilbo had in his pockets. That made Bilbo more curious about what he had. Gollum got angrier and came after Bilbo, who slipped the ring on his finger while feeling it in his pocket. Bilbo tripped trying to escape from Gollum, and Gollum went right by him, as if he were not there. Gollum talked to himself aloud, saying he was afraid the goblins would get Bilbo and the ring and use it to become invisible and get *him*.

7. How did Gandalf get rid of the wargs and goblins? Did it work?
    He lit pine cones on fire with his wand and threw them at the wargs. It worked to cause confusion and to get rid of some of the wolves, but it also set the woods on fire.

8. Beorn warned them about some things in Mirkwood. What?
    Beorn warned them about a black stream that crosses the path. He said it causes enchantment, a great drowsiness, and forgetfulness. He also warned them not to leave the path.

9. When did Bilbo first realize he could be courageous and bold?
    He first felt courageous and bold after he killed the spider and freed himself.

10. Why were the travelers actually glad to be captured by the wood elves?
    They were sick and tired and starving. Although they were prisoners, they at least received food and drink.

11. What was the Arkenstone? Trace who held it throughout the story.
    The Arkenstone was the most single most valuable item in the treasure pile. Smaug first had it among the treasures. Then Bilbo found it and hid it in his deepest pocket. Later, he gave it to Bard as a bargaining point with Thorin. In the end, it was buried with Thorin.

The Hobbit Answer Key Short Answer Test 1 page 3

12. What started the whole argument/war between the dwarves and the townspeople, represented by Bard?
    Bard asked Thorin to share the treasure with those who justly had a right to a portion of it. Thorin refused.

13. What did Bilbo miss at the end of the battle while he was knocked out?
    The eagles fought against the goblins. Beorn came and fought, found Thorin wounded and carried him to safety, returned tot he battle and killed Bolg, the goblin king. With Bolg dead, many goblins fled. They scattered and were killed by the elves and the armies who drove them away. Some goblins were eliminated by the perils of Mirkwood.

14. What, besides spoons, did Bilbo lose?
    He lost his reputation. He was an elf-friend, had the honor of dwarves and wizards, and was no longer quite respectable among the hobbits.

15. What were Gandalf's last words to Bilbo in this book?
    ". . . Surely you don't disbelieve the prophecies, because you had a hand in bringing them about yourself? You don't really suppose, do you, that all your adventures and escapes were managed by mere luck, just for your sole benefit? You are a very fine person, Mr. Baggins, and I am very fond of you; but you are only quite a little fellow in a wide world after all."

III. Essay
Choose the single most important point you think Tolkien was making in *The Hobbit*. State that point, explain why you chose it, and explain how it is made through the events and characters in the book.
    Answers will vary.

IV. Vocabulary
Choose ten of the vocabulary words to dictate to your students. Write them here if you wish.

SHORT ANSWER UNIT TEST 2 - *The Hobbit*

I. Matching

___ 1. Gandalf   A. raven
___ 2. Thorin   B. His grandfather was King of the Mountain
___ 3. Bilbo   C. dragon
___ 4. Dale   D. wolves
___ 5. Smaug   E. Thorin, Dori, Bofur, & Ori, for example
___ 6. Trolls   F. town ruins in the shadow of the mountain
___ 7. Dwarves   G. hobbit
___ 8. Elrond   H. King of the Elves
___ 9. Orcrist   I. killed the dragon
___ 10. Gollum   J. William, Bert & Tom
___ 11. Wargs   K. small, slimy water creature
___ 12. Eagles   L. sword
___ 13. Beorn   M. saved Thorin & Co. from goblins, wolves & fire
___ 14. Bard   N. wizard
___ 15. Roäc   O. bear-man

II. Short Answer

1. List three times Gandalf used magic to help the travelers.

2. What very useful items did Gandalf, Thorin, and Bilbo take from the trolls' cave? Why were these items important?

3. What big mistake did the travelers make in Mirkwood? Did it turn out to be a good mistake or a bad mistake in the end?

The Hobbit Short Answer Unit Test 2, page 2

4. Identify Lonely Mountain

5. Identify Lone Lands

6. Identify Esgaroth

7. List three ways Beorn helped the travelers.

8. Why were the incidents with the spiders important?

9. How did Bilbo find the ring, and how was it useful throughout the quest?

10. What characteristics does Bilbo have that make him a hero by the end of the story?

The Hobbit Short Answer Unit Test 2 page 3

III. Write a paragraph telling about each of these:

1. The Wood Elves

2. The Eagles

3. Roäc

4. Bard

5. Gollum

The Hobbit Short Answer Unit Test 2 page 4

IV. Vocabulary
    Listen to the vocabulary words and spell them.
    After you have spelled all the words, go back and write down the definitions.

1.

2.

3.

4.

5.

6.

7.

8.

9.

10.

ANSWER KEY SHORT ANSWER UNIT TEST 2 - *The Hobbit*

I. Matching

N	1. Gandalf	A. raven
B	2. Thorin	B. His grandfather was King of the Mountain
G	3. Bilbo	C. dragon
F	4. Dale	D. wolves
C	5. Smaug	E. Thorin, Dori, Bofur, & Ori, for example
J	6. Trolls	F. town ruins in the shadow of the mountain
E	7. Dwarves	G. hobbit
H	8. Elrond	H. King of the Elves
L	9. Orcrist	I. killed the dragon
K	10. Gollum	J. William, Bert & Tom
D	11. Wargs	K. small, slimy water creature
M	12. Eagles	L. sword
O	13. Beorn	M. saved Thorin & Co. from goblins, wolves & fire
I	14. Bard	N. wizard
A	15. Roäc	O. bear-man

II. Short Answer

1. List three times Gandalf used magic to help the travelers.

    He made the fire in the cavern blow up in smoke and sparks, which burned the goblins and created confusion, allowing the travelers to escape. He set the pine cones on fire to hold off the wolves and goblins. He mimicked the trolls' voices to get them arguing with each other until the sun came out and turned them to stone.

2. What very useful items did Gandalf, Thorin, and Bilbo take from the trolls' cave? Why were these items important?

    They took Orcrist, Glamdring, and a knife (which later became known as Sting).
    These weapons has special powers and were important in fighting the goblins.

4. What big mistake did the travelers make in Mirkwood? Did it turn out to be a good mistake or a bad mistake in the end?

    They left the path. Although it caused them many problems, it was good that they had left the path because the path no longer would have taken them out of Mirkwood anyway. By leaving the path, they unknowingly found the only way out of Mirkwood.

The Hobbit Answer Key Short Answer Unit Test 2, page 2

4. Identify Lonely Mountain

   That was the mountain where Smaug held the treasure, the mountain belonging to the dwarf King of the Mountain. It was the destination of the travelers.

5. Identify Lone Lands

   These were the first inhospitable lands the travelers encountered, the place where Bilbo first wanted to turn back.

6. Identify Esgaroth

   This was the lake town where the men lived, near Lonely Mountain.

7. List three ways Beorn helped the travelers.

   He gave them food, shelter, and transportation (ponies). He watch over them on their way, lurking nearby. He came to their aid in the Battle Of Five Armies.

8. Why were the incidents with the spiders important?

   Bilbo first became courageous and recognized his own ability to do brave deeds during the adventures with the spiders. Also, by rescuing the dwarves, he further gained their respect.

9. How did Bilbo find the ring, and how was it useful throughout the quest?

   He found it on the ground during his adventure with Gollum. It had the power to make the wearer invisible, which definitely came in handy. It enabled him to follow Gollum out of the cave, escape the goblins, sneak past guards, trick the spiders, and many other things. In the end, he put it on to try to remain safe during the Battle of the Five Armies, but he got hit in the head anyway, by accident.

10. What characteristics does Bilbo have that make him a hero by the end of the story?

    He is brave, smart, honorable, a peacemaker, one who seeks right and justice over personal good or glory.

The Hobbit Answer Key Short Answer Unit Test 2 page 3

III. Write a paragraph telling about each of these:

1. The Wood Elves
2. The Eagles
3. Roäc
4. Bard
5. Gollum

    The point here is to see what students have learned about each of these, to be able to correctly identify them and give some specific examples of their roles in the book.

IV. Vocabulary

    Choose ten vocabulary words to dictate to your students. Write them here if you wish.

MULTIPLE CHOICE UNIT TEST #1 - *The Hobbit*

I. Matching

___ 1. Mirkwood   A. food
___ 2. Orcrist   B. his grandfather was King of the Mountain
___ 3. Bilbo   C. dragon
___ 4. Dale   D. caused invisibility
___ 5. Bard   E. leader of the dwarves after Thorin
___ 6. Gandalf   F. bear-man
___ 7. Dain   G. hobbit
___ 8. Elrond   H. sword
___ 9. Thorin   I. killed the dragon
___ 10. Gollum   J. dark and gloomy forest
___ 11. Ring   K. small, slimy water creature
___ 12. Eagles   L. King of the Elves
___ 13. Beorn   M. saved Thorin & Co. from goblins, wolves & fire
___ 14. Smaug   N. wizard
___ 15. Cram   O. town ruins in the shadow of the mountain

II. Multiple Choice

1. Some of Bilbo's ancestors were Tooks. What influence did the Took genes have on Bilbo?
    A. They made him more of a home-body.
    B. They made him crabby and mean.
    C. They made him more adventurous than most other hobbits.
    D. They made him selfish.

2. What did the dwarves think of Bilbo in the beginning of the adventure? What did they think of him at the end of the story?
    A. They trusted Gandalf's judgement and thought he was a great burglar, and their opinions did not change throughout the book.
    B. They thought Bilbo was a terrible choice. They never had any confidence in him throughout the book. At the very end they reluctantly admitted he had done some good things on the quest.
    C. They doubted his abilities in the beginning and occasionally throughout the book, but as the quest unfolded, Bilbo proved himself to them. By the end of the book, they thought he was a great burglar and a hero.
    D. They used Bilbo from the beginning, knowing his capabilities even though he didn't know them himself. They always believed he could do the job, but never wanted to give him any credit for it. In the end they saw that they had been right all along but still refused to give him credit.

The Hobbit Multiple Choice Unit Test 1 page 2

3. What was the point of this quest and was this goal achieved?
    A. The point was to reclaim the lands and treasures of the dwarves from Smaug. Yes.
    B. The point was to help Bilbo prove himself so that he could be proud. Yes.
    C. The point was to defeat the goblins and wargs. No.
    D. The point was to make a bond between men and dwarves. No.

4. When did Bilbo first wish that he were back home?
    A. when they reached Mirkwood
    B. when they reached the Last Homely Home
    C. when they reached the Misty Mountain
    D. when they reached the Lone Lands

5. What important information did Elrond give the travelers on their way to Misty Mountain?
    A. He identified the swords Gandalf and Thorin had taken from the trolls' cave as being very old swords made for the Goblin-wars.
    B. He read the moon-letters to reveal the way to open the secret door on the side of the mountain.
    C. He told them not to leave the path.
    D. A & B

6. How did Bilbo discover the power of the ring?
    A. Gollum told him.
    B. It was inscribed on the ring.
    C. Bilbo slipped the ring on his finger and Gollum went right by him, as if he were not there.
    D. All of the above

7. How did Gandalf get rid of the wargs and goblins?
    A. He lit pine cones on fire with his wand and threw them at the wargs.
    B. He made smoke and sparks fly up and confuse them.
    C. He cast a spell on them, making them go away.
    D. He sent a thrush with a message to the eagles.

8. Beorn gave the travelers advice about Mirkwood. What was it?
    A. Follow the lights to food and water.
    B. Beware of the enchanted black water and never leave the path.
    C. Do not speak with any of the woodfolk.
    D. All of the above

The Hobbit Multiple Choice Unit Test 1 page 3

9. When did Bilbo first realize he could be courageous and bold?
    A. after he crossed the black water without incident
    B. after he went down Smaug's tunnel
    C. after he killed the spider and freed himself
    D. after he rested at Beorn's house

10. Why were the travelers actually glad to be captured by the wood elves?
    A. They knew the Elvenking would help them.
    B. They knew Gandalf would find them.
    C. The wood elves unknowingly helped them escape from the goblins.
    D. They were sick and tired and starving. Although they were prisoners, they at least received food and drink.

11. What was the Arkenstone?
    A. Thorin's sword
    B. the cup Bilbo stole from Smaug
    C. the stone at the front of Lonely Mountain
    D. the single most valuable piece of treasure

12. What started the whole argument/war between the dwarves and the townspeople, represented by Bard?
    A. Bard asked Thorin to share the treasure with those who justly had a right to a portion of it. Thorin refused.
    B. Bard insisted on having the Arkenstone. Thorin refused.
    C. Thorin found out that Bard had the Arkenstone and thought he had stolen it.
    D. Bard insisted that Thorin no longer had a right to the treasure, that it belonged to the townspeople. Thorin refused to give it up.

13. What did Bilbo miss at the end of the battle while he was knocked out?
    A. The eagles fought against the goblins.
    B. Beorn came and fought, found Thorin wounded and carried him to safety, returned to the battle and killed Bolg, the goblin king. With Bolg dead, many goblins fled.
    C. Goblins scattered and were killed by the elves and the armies who drove them away.
    D. All of the above

The Hobbit Multiple Choice Unit Test 1 page 3

14. What, besides spoons, did Bilbo lose?
    A. the Arkenstone
    B. his reputation
    C. Gandalf's friendship
    D. all of the above

15. What were Gandalf's last words to Bilbo in this book?
    A. Surely you don't disbelieve the prophecies, because you had a hand in bringing them about yourself?
    B. You don't really suppose, do you, that all your adventures and escapes were managed by mere luck, just for your sole benefit?
    C. You are a very fine person, Mr. Baggins, and I am very fond of you; but you are only quite a little fellow in a wide world after all.
    D. all of the above

The Hobbit Multiple Choice Unit Test 1 page 4

III. Essay   Compare and contrast Thorin and Bilbo.

The Hobbit Multiple Choice Unit Test 1 page 5

IV. Vocabulary

____ 1. INFURIATE   A. Thoroughly unpleasant
____ 2. QUAY   B. Acts of preying upon others
____ 3. LURE   C. In command of magic, spells & witchcraft
____ 4. PREFER   D. One who joins in planning or plotting
____ 5. ABOMINABLE   E. Relatives
____ 6. HOARD   F. Daring; bold
____ 7. WANING   G. Pantry or cupboards containing food stores
____ 8. CONSPIRATOR   H. Delay; get in the way of
____ 9. MEMOIRS   I. A gathered, hidden, or stored supply or treasure
____ 10. SUSPICION   J. Top; high point
____ 11. PLIGHT   K. To make angry; enrage
____ 12. HINDER   L. Gathering
____ 13. DELL   M. Entice; attract
____ 14. SORCEROUS   N. Narrative of experiences an author has lived through
____ 15. KIN   O. Going against the main current, especially in a swirling motion
____ 16. PINNACLE   P. Situation of difficulty
____ 17. MUSTERING   Q. To like better; rather
____ 18. AUDACIOUS   R. Wharf or reinforced bank where ships are loaded
____ 19. DEPREDATIONS   S. Small, secluded, wooded valley
____ 20. IMPLORE   T. Deep hatred
____ 21. GUARDIAN   U. Doubtful
____ 22. LARDERS   V. Thinking something exists, esp. something wrong, without any proof
____ 23. DUBIOUS   W. One who guards, protects or defends
____ 24. EDDYING   X. Ask or beg urgently
____ 25. ENMITY   Y. Lessening; going away; ending

MULTIPLE CHOICE UNIT TEST #2 - *The Hobbit*

I. Matching

___ 1. Mirkwood   A. killed the dragon
___ 2. Orcrist   B. dragon
___ 3. Bilbo   C. his grandfather was King of the Mountain
___ 4. Dale   D. bear-man
___ 5. Bard   E. dark and gloomy forest
___ 6. Gandalf   F. caused invisibility
___ 7. Dain   G. town ruins in the shadow of the mountain
___ 8. Elrond   H. saved Thorin & Co. from goblins, wolves & fire
___ 9. Thorin   I. food
___ 10. Gollum   J. leader of the dwarves after Thorin
___ 11. Ring   K. King of the Elves
___ 12. Eagles   L. small, slimy water creature
___ 13. Beorn   M. sword
___ 14. Smaug   N. wizard
___ 15. Cram   O. hobbit

II. Multiple Choice

1. Which was a time Gandalf did NOT use magic to help the travelers.
    A. when he made the fire in the cavern blow up in smoke and sparks, which burned the goblins and created confusion, allowing the travelers to escape.
    B. when he set the pine cones on fire to hold off the wolves and goblins.
    C. when he mimicked the trolls' voices to get them arguing with each other until the sun came out and turned them to stone.
    D. none of the above

2. What items did Gandalf, Thorin, and Bilbo take from the trolls' cave?
    A. They took swords and a knife.
    B. They took food.
    C. They took treasure.
    D. all of the above

4. What big mistake did the travelers make in Mirkwood?
    A. They killed the hart.
    B. They drank the water.
    C. They left the path.
    D. They kept the ponies.

The Hobbit Multiple Choice Unit Test 2 page 2

4. Identify Lonely Mountain
   A. the mountain where the Elvenking lived
   B. the mountain where Smaug held the treasure
   C. the mountain where Beorn lived
   D. the mountain under which the goblins lived

5. Identify Lone Lands
   A. the first inhospitable lands the travelers encountered
   B. the lands of the Elvenking
   C. the lands rightfully belonging to the King of the Mountain
   D. the lands belonging to the men of the lake

6. Identify Esgaroth
   A. the Elvenking
   B. the lake town where the men lived
   C. the goblin king Thorin's grandfather killed
   D. Thorin's sword

7. He gave them food, shelter, and transportation (ponies). He watch over them on their way, lurking nearby. He came to their aid in the Battle Of Five Armies. Who is he?
   A. Elrond
   B. Gandalf
   C. Beorn
   D. Dain

8. Why were the incidents with the spiders important?
   A. Bilbo first became courageous and recognized his own ability to do brave deeds during the adventures with the spiders.
   B. By rescuing the dwarves from the spiders, Bilbo further gained their respect.
   C. Thorin & Co. got much needed food and supplies.
   D. A & B

9. In what event was the ring NOT of much use to Bilbo?
   A. during the Battle of Five Armies
   B. during the escape from the spiders
   C. during the escape from the goblins
   D. none of the above

The Hobbit Multiple Choice Unit Test 2 page 3

10. What characteristic does Bilbo NOT have by the end of the story?
    A. He is brave.
    B. He is a peacemaker.
    C. He seeks personal good and glory.
    D. He confident.

11. What was the Arkenstone?
    A. Thorin's sword
    B. the single most valuable piece of treasure
    C. the stone at the front of Lonely Mountain
    D. the cup Bilbo stole from Smaug

12. What started the whole argument/war between the dwarves and the townspeople, represented by Bard?
    A. Bard asked Thorin to share the treasure with those who justly had a right to a portion of it. Thorin refused.
    B. Bard insisted on having the Arkenstone. Thorin refused.
    C. Thorin found out that Bard had the Arkenstone and thought he had stolen it.
    D. Bard insisted that Thorin no longer had a right to the treasure, that it belonged to the townspeople. Thorin refused to give it up.

13. What did Bilbo miss at the end of the battle while he was knocked out?
    A. The wargs turned against the goblins.
    B. Beorn came and fought, found Thorin wounded and carried him to safety, returned to the battle and killed Bolg, the goblin king. With Bolg dead, many goblins fled.
    C. Thorin killed Bolg, the goblin king, but was mortally wounded in the process.
    D. All of the above

14. What, in the end, did Bilbo lose?
    A. the Arkenstone
    B. his home
    C. his reputation
    D. all of the above

15. What were Gandalf's last words to Bilbo?
    A. Don't mind losing your home, Bilbo. After all, material things don't matter.
    B. And now, my dear Mr. Baggins, farewell until the next adventure.
    C. You are only quite a little fellow in a wide world after all.
    D. all of the above

The Hobbit Multiple Choice Unit Test 2 page 4

III. Essay

Is Bilbo's use of the ring at the end of the story in the Battle of Five armies an intelligent act or an act of cowardice? Consider Bilbo's role in the story and either defend or condemn his use of the ring in the Battle of Five Armies.

The Hobbit Multiple Choice Unit Test 2 page 5

IV. Vocabulary

____ 1. QUAY   A. Ridiculous
____ 2. WILY   B. Lift up
____ 3. LOATHSOME   C. One who guards, protects or defends
____ 4. ENMITY   D. Deep hatred
____ 5. DROUGHT   E. Ask or beg urgently
____ 6. MARAUDING   F. Pantry or cupboards containing food stores
____ 7. QUEST   G. Dangerous
____ 8. IMPENETRABLE   H. Rest
____ 9. ANTIQUITY   I. Delay; get in the way of
____ 10. REPOSE   J. One who joins in planning or plotting
____ 11. DUBIOUS   K. Long period of time with no rain
____ 12. LARDERS   L. Unavoidable
____ 13. RUNES   M. Doubtful
____ 14. GUARDIAN   N. Repulsive; disgusting
____ 15. ABSURD   O. Thoroughly unpleasant
____ 16. WANING   P. Lessening; going away; ending
____ 17. SORCEROUS   Q. Words written in ancient Germanic letters
____ 18. ABOMINABLE   R. Quality of being very old or ancient
____ 19. HINDER   S. Wandering in search of something to steal
____ 20. INEVITABLE   T. Search
____ 21. PERILOUS   U. Wharf or reinforced bank where ships are loaded
____ 22. PINNACLE   V. Can't be pierced or entered through
____ 23. CONSPIRATOR   W. Calculating; plotting
____ 24. IMPLORE   X. Top; high point
____ 25. HOIST   Y. In command of magic, spells & witchcraft

ANSWER KEYS MULTIPLE CHOICE UNIT TESTS - *The Hobbit*
Test 1 answers are in the left-hand column. Test 2 answers are in the right-hand column.

I. Matching	II. Multiple Choice	IV. Vocabulary
1. J E	1. C D	1. K U
2. H M	2. C D	2. R W
3. G O	3. A C	3. M N
4. O G	4. D B	4. Q D
5. I A	5. D A	5. A K
6. N N	6. C B	6. I S
7. E J	7. A C	7. Y T
8. L K	8. B D	8. D V
9. B C	9. C A	9. N R
10. K L	10. D C	10. V H
11. D F	11. D B	11. P M
12. M H	12. A A	12. H F
13. F D	13. D B	13. S Q
14. C B	14. B C	14. C C
15. A I	15. D C	15. E A
		16. J P
		17. L Y
		18. F O
		19. B I
		20. X L
		21. W G
		22. G X
		23. U J
		24. O E
		25. T B

ADVANCED SHORT ANSWER UNIT TEST - *The Hobbit*

I. Matching

___ 1. Gandalf   A. raven
___ 2. Thorin   B. His grandfather was King of the Mountain
___ 3. Bilbo   C. dragon
___ 4. Dale   D. wolves
___ 5. Smaug   E. Thorin, Dori, Bofur, & Ori, for example
___ 6. Trolls   F. town ruins in the shadow of the mountain
___ 7. Dwarves   G. hobbit
___ 8. Elrond   H. King of the Elves
___ 9. Orcrist   I. killed the dragon
___ 10. Gollum   J. William, Bert & Tom
___ 11. Wargs   K. small, slimy water creature
___ 12. Eagles   L. sword
___ 13. Beorn   M. saved Thorin & Co. from goblins, wolves & fire
___ 14. Bard   N. wizard
___ 15. Roäc   O. bear-man

II. Short Answer

1. Compare and contrast Thorin and Bilbo.

2. Explain when and why Bilbo uses the ring. Give at least three instances.

The Hobbit Advanced Short Answer Unit Test page 2

3. Describe four main events that show Bilbo's growth as a character throughout the book. Explain what each event shows about Bilbo's character.

4. Describe the role of each of the following characters. What did they do, and what was the use of each in the novel?

a. Beorn

b. Gollum

c. Bard

d. Master

e. Roäc

The Hobbit Advanced Short Answer Unit Test page 3

5. How is *The Hobbit* a book about good versus evil?

6. Give at least 3 examples of when things were not as they appeared to be in *The Hobbit*.

7. What is Gandalf's use as a character in the book? He is in at the beginning and end, but leaves through the middle sections. Why?

8. "Songs" are used throughout the book. Why?

The Hobbit Advanced Short Answer Unit Test page 4

III. Essay

Tolkien's book *The Hobbit* is very popular. Explain why. What elements in the story make it so appealing? Give specific examples from the book to support your statements.

The Hobbit Advanced Short Answer Unit Test page 5

IV. Vocabulary

Listen to the vocabulary words and write them down. After you have written down all the words, write a paragraph in which you use all the words. The paragraph must in some way relate to *The Hobbit*.

ANSWER SHEET - *The Hobbit*
Multiple Choice Unit Tests

I. Matching	II. Multiple Choice	IV. Vocabulary
1. ___	1. ___	1. ___
2. ___	2. ___	2. ___
3. ___	3. ___	3. ___
4. ___	4. ___	4. ___
5. ___	5. ___	5. ___
6. ___	6. ___	6. ___
7. ___	7. ___	7. ___
8. ___	8. ___	8. ___
	9. ___	9. ___
	10. ___	10. ___
	11. ___	11. ___
		12. ___
		13. ___
		14. ___
		15. ___
		16. ___
		17. ___
		18. ___
		19. ___
		20. ___

UNIT RESOURCE MATERIALS

BULLETIN BOARD IDEAS - *The Hobbit*

1. Save a space for students' best writing. Make a nice border. Cut out letters THE BEST or YOU'RE THE TOPS! with a cut-out top hat -- whatever title you want to show the meaning of the space. Staple up the best writing samples (or quizzes or whatever you have graded) on colorful paper.

2. Place background paper on the bulletin board with a simple title THE HOBBIT. Invite students throughout the unit to draw their favorite characters or scenes or write their favorite quotes from the book onto the bulletin board. Students can either draw directly on the board or post things they write or draw on paper.

3. Draw one of the word search puzzles onto the bulletin board. (Be sure to enlarge it.) Write the key words to one side. Invite students to take their pens or markers and find the words before and/or after class (or perhaps this could be an activity for students who finish their work early).

4. Post articles about *The Hobbit*, Tolkien, and/or Tolkien's other works on the board.

5. Invite students to explore web sites relating to Tolkien's works. Make an Internet connection bulletin board where students can post reviews of sites they have visited.

6. Post the names of all the characters onto the bulletin board. Invite students to write words or phrases to tell about each character as they read the book. Maybe you could take a few minutes after reviewing the study questions for each section and ask for words about characters in that section. Write them clearly on the board to try to help students remember the characters and what they do. Including names of places would be helpful, too.

7. Make a bulletin board about other fantasy books students might enjoy. Use book jackets or write short summaries of the books as teasers on colorful construction paper.

EXTRA ACTIVITIES

One of the difficulties in teaching a novel is that all students don't read at the same speed. One student who likes to read may take the book home and finish it in a day or two. Sometimes a few students finish the in-class assignments early. The problem, then, is finding suitable extra activities for students.

One thing that helps is to keep a little library in the classroom. For this unit on *The Hobbit*, you might check out from the school library other books by Tolkien. A biography of the author would be interesting for some students. You may include other related books and articles about magic, ghosts and goblins, wars and battles, or any of the other topics listed in the nonfiction assignment page of this unit (Lesson Twelve).

Other things you may keep on hand are puzzles. We have made some relating directly to *The Hobbit* for you. Feel free to duplicate them for your class.

Some students may like to draw. You might devise a contest or allow some extra-credit grade for students who draw characters or scenes from *The Hobbit*. Note, too, that if the students do not want to keep their drawings you may pick up some extra bulletin board materials this way. If you have a contest and you supply the prize (a CD or something like that perhaps), you could, possibly, make the drawing itself a non-refundable entry fee.

The pages which follow contain games, puzzles and worksheets. The keys, when appropriate, immediately follow the puzzle or worksheet. There are two main groups of activities: one group for the unit; that is, generally relating to the *Hobbit* text, and another group of activities related strictly to the *Hobbit* vocabulary.

Directions for the games, puzzles and worksheets are self-explanatory. The object here is to provide you with extra materials you may use in any way you choose.

MORE ACTIVITIES - *The Hobbit*

1. Pick a chapter or scene with a great deal of dialogue and have the students act it out on a stage. (Perhaps you could assign various scenes to different groups of students so more than one scene could be acted and more students could participate.)

2. Show a film version of *The Hobbit* to the class after you have completed reading the novel. Have students evaluate the movie and compare/contrast it with the book. If the students have tried writing a chapter into a scene in a play, you may wish to discuss how the problems they encountered in changing the form were handled in the movie.

3. Have students design a book cover (front and back and inside flaps) for *The Hobbit*.

4. Have students design a bulletin board (ready to be put up; not just sketched) for *The Hobbit*.

5. There are literally over a hundred web sites related to Tolkien's works on the Internet, as of the date of this publication. Search a list of sites and assign one site for each of your students to explore and report about. Students can swap information about fun or particularly informative sites.

6. Use some of the related topics (noted earlier for an in-class library) as topics for research, reports or written papers, or as topics for guest speakers.

7. See the bulletin board ideas page for some additional activities.

8. Organize (or have students organize) a *Hobbit* Tea Party. Have students dress up as characters in the book, decorate your room like Bilbo's house, and serve foods mentioned in the book.

9. Invite a magician to come and perform for your class.

WORD SEARCH - The Hobbit

```
N I L B O G B R F C T R S M A P P Q G R
E T H O R I N R I R I V W M K Y H D A F
C Z C S L S A K V T B W O B E G Q A N F
K L U E E W G T E W B Z R S A L Y I D B
L P P L D M I R K W O O D D P R L N A M
A X G D C L C E E B H O S B U I R R L L
C A M D V E L T L E H E D B B R D E F L
E N T I S G B I G C N X M E Y L I E L X
S I B R S B B B G O L O R W L P K N R S
B A E T D T V V C H B C I I E V S H P S
Y T O W A V Y E G P T T V L M T E Y O G
F N R Y L E N O L A J S E L O R H S N L
E U N W E I C R A M R Y N I H E S G I R
K O P I P E W A R G S K D A T E U S E V
Q M T R E A S U R E H F E M Y S R W S W
W S G Q F T E W X D G B L N G M H W B T
P H H M E M H L F K N F L U S J T L Q H
S A A K T M D C V Y I R A W M T A S K W
L D C Z O N C D T E T M H Z O C O R E H
B O A T O O R C R I S T O L K I E N Y S
P W N R K G D I O O A S W M E I G S E W
M L L E M K N S L P A T Q Q D X N M V V
P E G C Q G O L L U M C H T O R A G S E
```

ARKENSTONE	DURIN	KING	PONIES	THORIN
AZOG	DWARF	LIGHTS	RIDDLES	THRUSHES
BARD	EAGLES	LONE	RING	TOLKIEN
BARRELS	ELROND	LONELY	RIVENDELL	TOOK
BEORN	ELVES	MAP	ROAC	TREASURE
BILBO	ESGAROTH	MIRKWOOD	SECRET	TREES
BITER	FIVE	MISTY	SHADOW	TROLL
BLACK	GANDALF	MOUNTAIN	SMAUG	WARGS
BOAT	GOBLIN	NECKLACE	SMELL	WILLIAM
BOMBUR	GOLLUM	ORCRIST	SMOKE	WOODELVES
CRAM	GREEN	PATH	SPIDERS	
CUP	HOBBIT	PINECONES	STING	
DAIN	HOMELY	PIPE	STONE	
DALE	KEY	POCKETS	SWORDS	

WORD SEARCH ANSWER KEY - The Hobbit

ARKENSTONE	DURIN	KING	PONIES	THORIN
AZOG	DWARF	LIGHTS	RIDDLES	THRUSHES
BARD	EAGLES	LONE	RING	TOLKIEN
BARRELS	ELROND	LONELY	RIVENDELL	TOOK
BEORN	ELVES	MAP	ROAC	TREASURE
BILBO	ESGAROTH	MIRKWOOD	SECRET	TREES
BITER	FIVE	MISTY	SHADOW	TROLL
BLACK	GANDALF	MOUNTAIN	SMAUG	WARGS
BOAT	GOBLIN	NECKLACE	SMELL	WILLIAM
BOMBUR	GOLLUM	ORCRIST	SMOKE	WOODELVES
CRAM	GREEN	PATH	SPIDERS	
CUP	HOBBIT	PINECONES	STING	
DAIN	HOMELY	PIPE	STONE	
DALE	KEY	POCKETS	SWORDS	

CROSSWORD *The Hobbit*

CROSSWORD CLUES - *The Hobbit*

ACROSS

1. The Foe Hammer
4. Misty or Lonely
6. The ___ in Bilbo made him adventurous
8. Used to cross the black water
9. Bilbo took this item, which made Smaug angry
12. Smaug's puff
16. Wizard
19. Gollum couldn't guess what was in Bilbo's
20. Bert or Tom, for example
21. Dwarves thought these creatures were foolish
24. Raven; son of Carc
25. ___ & Beater; goblin name for Orcrist
27. Bear-man
29. Evil wolves
30. King of the Elves
32. last ___ Home; Elrond's home
33. Gandalf and Thorin took ___ from the trolls' cave
37. Gandalf gave Thorin this and a key
39. Got wet in the enchanted black water
40. Leader of the dwarves after Thorin
43. ___ River; river in Mirkwood
45. Bilbo, for example
46. Saved Thorin & Co. from the wargs & goblins
47. Bilbo's name for his knife
48. Travelers looked for the ___ entrance to the mountain

DOWN

1. ___ Dragon Inn
2. Dwalin, Bifur or Dori, for example
3. Bilbo's gift to the Elvenking to repay his hospitality
5. Greatest single treasure
6. His grandfather was King of the Mountain
7. Elrond was ___ of the Elves
10. Bilbo's smoking device
11. The Goblin Cleaver
13. ___ Mountain
14. It opened the secret door in the mountain
15. Gandalf lit them on fire and threw them at wargs
17. Goblin that killed Thorin's grandfather
18. Town ruins in the shadow of the mountain
20. Thorin & Co. climbed in them to avoid the wargs
22. ___ Lands; where Bilbo first wished he were home
23. Bilbo's showed even when he wore the ring
26. Gollum's birthday present that Bilbo found
28. Land of the elves
31. Tame messenger birds
33. Trolls turned to ___ in the sun
34. Bilbo & Gollum's game
35. Dragon
38. Never leave the ___ in Mirkwood
39. Mr. Baggins
41. Travelers left the path to see what was at these
42. Battle of ___ Armies
44. Biscuit-like food

CROSSWORD *The Hobbit*

MATCHING WORKSHEET 1 - The Hobbit

___ 1. BILBO A. Captured the dwarves & actually saved them
___ 2. GREEN B. It opened the secret door in the mountain
___ 3. PONIES C. Bilbo's name for his knife
___ 4. WOODELVES D. Last ____ Home; Elrond's home
___ 5. MAP E. The ____ in Bilbo made him adventurous
___ 6. STING F. King of the Elves
___ 7. HOMELY G. Old watch post on SW side of mountain
___ 8. HOBBIT H. Got wet in the enchanted black water
___ 9. RAVENHILL I. Bilbo took this item, which made Smaug angry
___10. ELVES J. Goblin that killed Thorin's grandfather
___11. WILLIAM K. Trolls turned to ___ in the sun
___12. EAGLES L. Azog, for example
___13. SPIDERS M. Bilbo, for example
___14. THRUSHES N. Saved Thorin & Co. from the wargs & goblins
___15. STONE O. Smaug's sense of ___ was keen
___16. BOMBUR P. Troll who caught Bilbo trying to pick his pocket
___17. KEY Q. Tame messenger birds
___18. PIPE R. Mr. Baggins
___19. CUP S. Bilbo's showed even when he wore the ring
___20. GOBLIN T. Bilbo's smoking device
___21. ELROND U. Beorn loaned these as transportation for the travelers
___22. SHADOW V. Dwarves thought these creatures were foolish
___23. TOOK W. Killing one gave Bilbo confidence
___24. SMELL X. Gandalf gave Thorin this and a key
___25. AZOG Y. ____ Dragon Inn

MATCHING WORKSHEET ANSWER KEY 1 - The Hobbit

R - 1. BILBO   A. Captured the dwarves & actually saved them
Y - 2. GREEN   B. It opened the secret door in the mountain
U - 3. PONIES   C. Bilbo's name for his knife
A - 4. WOODELVES   D. Last ____ Home; Elrond's home
X - 5. MAP   E. The ____ in Bilbo made him adventurous
C - 6. STING   F. King of the Elves
D - 7. HOMELY   G. Old watch post on SW side of mountain
M - 8. HOBBIT   H. Got wet in the enchanted black water
G - 9. RAVENHILL   I. Bilbo took this item, which made Smaug angry
V - 10. ELVES   J. Goblin that killed Thorin's grandfather
P - 11. WILLIAM   K. Trolls turned to ____ in the sun
N - 12. EAGLES   L. Azog, for example
W - 13. SPIDERS   M. Bilbo, for example
Q - 14. THRUSHES   N. Saved Thorin & Co. from the wargs & goblins
K - 15. STONE   O. Smaug's sense of ____ was keen
H - 16. BOMBUR   P. Troll who caught Bilbo trying to pick his pocket
B - 17. KEY   Q. Tame messenger birds
T - 18. PIPE   R. Mr. Baggins
I - 19. CUP   S. Bilbo's showed even when he wore the ring
L - 20. GOBLIN   T. Bilbo's smoking device
F - 21. ELROND   U. Beorn loaned these as transportation for the travelers
S - 22. SHADOW   V. Dwarves thought these creatures were foolish
E - 23. TOOK   W. Killing one gave Bilbo confidence
O - 24. SMELL   X. Gandalf gave Thorin this and a key
J - 25. AZOG   Y. ____ Dragon Inn

MATCHING WORKSHEET 2 - The Hobbit

___ 1. SWORDS	A. ____ Lands; where Bilbo first wished he were home

___ 2. TOLKIEN	B. Author

___ 3. ELVES	C. Troll who caught Bilbo trying to pick his pocket

___ 4. PONIES	D. Never leave the path in this place

___ 5. LONE	E. Greatest single treasure

___ 6. TREASURE	F. Lake town

___ 7. BOAT	G. King of the Elves

___ 8. SPIDERS	H. His grandfather was King of the Mountain

___ 9. TREES	I. Dwarves thought these creatures were foolish

___10. MIRKWOOD	J. Bilbo's smoking device

___11. ELROND	K. The Goblin Cleaver

___12. GOBLIN	L. Bilbo & Gollum's game

___13. WILLIAM	M. Gandalf lit them on fire & threw them at wargs

___14. ESGAROTH	N. Used to cross the black water

___15. TOOK	O. Smaug slept on it

___16. ORCRIST	P. Beorn loaned these as transportation for the travelers

___17. BLACK	Q. Azog, for example

___18. PINECONES	R. ____ River; river in Mirkwood

___19. FIVE	S. Thorin & Co. climbed in them to avoid wargs

___20. PIPE	T. Killing one gave Bilbo confidence

___21. RIDDLES	U. Captured the dwarves & actually saved them

___22. THORIN	V. The Foe Hammer

___23. WOODELVES	W. Battle of ____ Armies

___24. ARKENSTONE	X. Gandalf and Thorin took ____ from the trolls' cave

___25. GLAMDRING	Y. The ____ in Bilbo made him adventurous

MATCHING WORKSHEET ANSWER KEY 2 - The Hobbit

X - 1. SWORDS	A.	____ Lands; where Bilbo first wished he were home
B - 2. TOLKIEN	B.	Author
I - 3. ELVES	C.	Troll who caught Bilbo trying to pick his pocket
P - 4. PONIES	D.	Never leave the path in this place
A - 5. LONE	E.	Greatest single treasure
O - 6. TREASURE	F.	Lake town
N - 7. BOAT	G.	King of the Elves
T - 8. SPIDERS	H.	His grandfather was King of the Mountain
S - 9. TREES	I.	Dwarves thought these creatures were foolish
D -10. MIRKWOOD	J.	Bilbo's smoking device
G -11. ELROND	K.	The Goblin Cleaver
Q -12. GOBLIN	L.	Bilbo & Gollum's game
C -13. WILLIAM	M.	Gandalf lit them on fire & threw them at wargs
F -14. ESGAROTH	N.	Used to cross the black water
Y -15. TOOK	O.	Smaug slept on it
K -16. ORCRIST	P.	Beorn loaned these as transportation for the travelers
R -17. BLACK	Q.	Azog, for example
M -18. PINECONES	R.	____ River; river in Mirkwood
W -19. FIVE	S.	Thorin & Co. climbed in them to avoid wargs
J - 20. PIPE	T.	Killing one gave Bilbo confidence
L -21. RIDDLES	U.	Captured the dwarves & actually saved them
H -22. THORIN	V.	The Foe Hammer
U -23. WOODELVES	W.	Battle of ____ Armies
E -24. ARKENSTONE	X.	Gandalf and Thorin took ____ from the trolls' cave
V -25. GLAMDRING	Y.	The ____ in Bilbo made him adventurous

JUGGLE LETTER 1 - The Hobbit

1. NEONERACRMC = 1. _____
   Council of Wizards drove the ____ out of southern Mirkwood

2. OBIHTB = 2. _____
   Bilbo, for example

3. ADSHWO = 3. _____
   Bilbo's showed even when he wore the ring

4. RIESDSP = 4. _____
   Killing one gave Bilbo confidence

5. RTHASEGO = 5. _____
   Lake town

6. APM = 6. _____
   Gandalf gave Thorin this and a key

7. MLHYEO = 7. _____
   Last ____ Home; Elrond's home

8. AIDN = 8. _____
   Leader of the dwarves after Thorin

9. SREUETAR = 9. _____
   Smaug slept on it

10. OAZG =10. _____
    Goblin that killed Thorin's grandfather

11. KODWMRIO =11. _____
    Never leave the path in this place

12. UEHHSTSR =12. _____
    Tame messenger birds

13. LLGOMU =13. _____
    Pale-eyed water creature

14. NLVRHAEIL =14. _____
    Old watch post on SW side of mountain

15. DOSSWR =15. _____
    Gandalf and Thorin took ___ from the trolls' cave

16. GSITN =16. _____
Bilbo's name for his knife

17. RACM =17. _____
Biscuit-like food

18. GEELAS =18. _____
Saved Thorin & Co. from the wargs & goblins

19. LLEMS =19. _____
Smaug's sense of ___ was keen

20. ETRSE =20. _____
Thorin & Co. climbed in them to avoid wargs

21. IYSTM =21. _____
_____ Mountains

22. OOTK =22. _____
The ____ in Bilbo made him adventurous

23. RUDNI =23. _____
Elf New Year; ___'s Day

24. NIRG =24. _____
Gollum's birthday present that Bilbo found

25. ESDDLRI =25. _____
Bilbo & Gollum's game

26. EVIF =26. _____
Battle of ____ Armies

27. WFADR =27. _____
Dwalin, Bifur or Dori, for example

28. NTOSE =28. _____
Trolls turned to ___ in the sun

29. IONEPESCN =29. _____
Gandalf lit them on fire & threw them at wargs

30. UPC =30. _____
Bilbo took this item, which made Smaug angry

31. RLLOT =31. _____
Bert or Tom, for example

32. CEALCKEN =32. _____
Bilbo's gift to Elvenking to repay his hospitality

33. BOLBI =33. _____
Mr. Baggins

34. LFAGNAD =34. _____
Wizard

35. AELD =35. _____
Town ruins in the shadow of the mountain

JUGGLE LETTER ANSWER KEY 1 - The Hobbit

1. ABDR = 1. BARD
   Killed Smaug with a black arrow

2. COSEPKT = 2. POCKETS
   Gollum couldn't guess what was in Bilbo's ___

3. NLEO = 3. LONE
   ___ Lands; where Bilbo first wished he were home

4. RIRSTCO = 4. ORCRIST
   The Goblin Cleaver

5. MKSEO = 5. SMOKE
   Smaug's puff

6. LSEEV = 6. ELVES
   Dwarves thought these creatures were foolish

7. CRTEES = 7. SECRET
   Travelers looked for the ___ entrance to the mountain

8. EPIP = 8. PIPE
   Bilbo's smoking device

9. ANGGRDLIM = 9. GLAMDRING
   The Foe Hammer

10. ENRGE =10. GREEN
    ___ Dragon Inn

11. LGINOB =11. GOBLIN
    Azog, for example

12. OARC =12. ROAC
    Raven; son of Carc

13. NAUIOMNT =13. MOUNTAIN
    Misty or Lonely

14. SLAEBRR =14. BARRELS
    Escape vehicles to take dwarves away from woodelves

15. ILHSTG =15. LIGHTS
    Travelers left the path to see what was at these

16. GSITN	=16.	STING
		Bilbo's name for his knife
17. RACM	=17.	CRAM
		Biscuit-like food
18. GEELAS	=18.	EAGLES
		Saved Thorin & Co. from the wargs & goblins
19. LLEMS	=19.	SMELL
		Smaug's sense of ___ was keen
20. ETRSE	=20.	TREES
		Thorin & Co. climbed in them to avoid wargs
21. IYSTM	=21.	MISTY
		_____ Mountains
22. OOTK	=22.	TOOK
		The ___ in Bilbo made him adventurous
23. RUDNI	=23.	DURIN
		Elf New Year; ___'s Day
24. NIRG	=24.	RING
		Gollum's birthday present that Bilbo found
25. ESDDLRI	=25.	RIDDLES
		Bilbo & Gollum's game
26. EVIF	=26.	FIVE
		Battle of ____ Armies
27. WFADR	=27.	DWARF
		Dwalin, Bifur or Dori, for example
28. NTOSE	=28.	STONE
		Trolls turned to ___ in the sun
29. IONEPESCN	=29.	PINECONES
		Gandalf lit them on fire & threw them at wargs
30. UPC	=30.	CUP
		Bilbo took this item, which made Smaug angry
31. RLLOT	=31.	TROLL
		Bert or Tom, for example
32. CEALCKEN	=32.	NECKLACE
		Bilbo's gift to Elvenking to repay his hospitality

33. BOLBI =33. BILBO
Mr. Baggins

34. LFAGNAD =34. GANDALF
Wizard

35. AELD =35. DALE
Town ruins in the shadow of the mountain

JUGGLE LETTER 2 - The Hobbit

1. ABDR = 1. _____
   Killed Smaug with a black arrow

2. COSEPKT = 2. _____
   Gollum couldn't guess what was in Bilbo's ___

3. NLEO = 3. _____
   ____ Lands; where Bilbo first wished he were home

4. RIRSTCO = 4. _____
   The Goblin Cleaver

5. MKSEO = 5. _____
   Smaug's puff

6. LSEEV = 6. _____
   Dwarves thought these creatures were foolish

7. CRTEES = 7. _____
   Travelers looked for the ___ entrance to the mountain

8. EPIP = 8. _____
   Bilbo's smoking device

9. ANGGRDLIM = 9. _____
   The Foe Hammer

10. ENRGE =10. _____
    _____ Dragon Inn

11. LGINOB =11. _____
    Azog, for example

12. OARC =12. _____
    Raven; son of Carc

13. NAUIOMNT =13. _____
    Misty or Lonely

14. SLAEBRR =14. _____
    Escape vehicles to take dwarves away from woodelves

15. ILHSTG =15. _____
    Travelers left the path to see what was at these

16. TNRAOKEESN =16. _____
Greatest single treasure

17. NKIG =17. _____
Elrond was ___ of the Elves

18. DWVOLESOE =18. _____
Captured the dwarves & actually saved them

19. SENIPO =19. _____
Beorn loaned these as transportation for the travelers

20. OBUBRM =20. _____
Got wet in the enchanted black water

21. OBTA =21. _____
Used to cross the black water

22. NHOTIR =22. _____
His grandfather was King of the Mountain

23. ONERB =23. _____
Bear-man

24. RSGWA =24. _____
Evil wolves

25. NEIRLLEVD =25. _____
Land of the elves

26. KALCB =26. _____
____ River; river in Mirkwood

27. TPAH =27. _____
Never leave the ___ in Mirkwood

28. YEOLLN =28. _____
___ Mountain; where Smaug lived

29. OERLND =29. _____
King of the Elves

30. AILMWLI =30. _____
Troll who caught Bilbo trying to pick his pocket

31. KNTOILE =31. _____
Author

32. MSUGA =32. _____
Dragon

33. IBRET   =33. _____
                        ___ & Beater; goblin names for Orcrist & Glamdring

34. YEK   =34. _____
                        It opened the secret door in the mountain

JUGGLE LETTER ANSWER KEY 2 - The Hobbit

1. ABDR = 1. BARD
   Killed Smaug with a black arrow

2. COSEPKT = 2. POCKETS
   Gollum couldn't guess what was in Bilbo's ___

3. NLEO = 3. LONE
   ___ Lands; where Bilbo first wished he were home

4. RIRSTCO = 4. ORCRIST
   The Goblin Cleaver

5. MKSEO = 5. SMOKE
   Smaug's puff

6. LSEEV = 6. ELVES
   Dwarves thought these creatures were foolish

7. CRTEES = 7. SECRET
   Travelers looked for the ___ entrance to the mountain

8. EPIP = 8. PIPE
   Bilbo's smoking device

9. ANGGRDLIM = 9. GLAMDRING
   The Foe Hammer

10. ENRGE =10. GREEN
    ___ Dragon Inn

11. LGINOB =11. GOBLIN
    Azog, for example

12. OARC =12. ROAC
    Raven; son of Carc

13. NAUIOMNT =13. MOUNTAIN
    Misty or Lonely

14. SLAEBRR =14. BARRELS
    Escape vehicles to take dwarves away from woodelves

15. ILHSTG =15. LIGHTS
    Travelers left the path to see what was at these

16. TNRAOKEESN =16. ARKENSTONE
Greatest single treasure

17. NKIG =17. KING
Elrond was ___ of the Elves

18. DWVOLESOE =18. WOODELVES
Captured the dwarves & actually saved them

19. SENIPO =19. PONIES
Beorn loaned these as transportation for the travelers

20. OBUBRM =20. BOMBUR
Got wet in the enchanted black water

21. OBTA =21. BOAT
Used to cross the black water

22. NHOTIR =22. THORIN
His grandfather was King of the Mountain

23. ONERB =23. BEORN
Bear-man

24. RSGWA =24. WARGS
Evil wolves

25. NEIRLLEVD =25. RIVENDELL
Land of the elves

26. KALCB =26. BLACK
___ River; river in Mirkwood

27. TPAH =27. PATH
Never leave the ___ in Mirkwood

28. YEOLLN =28. LONELY
___ Mountain; where Smaug lived

29. OERLND =29. ELROND
King of the Elves

30. AILMWLI =30. WILLIAM
Troll who caught Bilbo trying to pick his pocket

31. KNTOILE =31. TOLKIEN
Author

32. MSUGA =32. SMAUG
Dragon

33. IBRET =33. BITER
___ & Beater; goblin names for Orcrist & Glamdring

34. YEK =34. KEY
It opened the secret door in the mountain

UNIT WORD LIST *The Hobbit*

Arkenstone	Greatest single treasure
Azog	Goblin that killed Thorin's grandfather
Bard	Killed Smaug with a black arrow
Barrels	Escape vehicles to take dwarves away from woodelves
Beorn	Bear-man
Bilbo	Mr. Baggins
Biter	___ & Beater; goblin names for Orcrist and Glamdring
Black	___ River; river in Mirkwood
Boat	Used to cross the black water
Bombur	Got wet in the enchanted black water
Cram	Biscuit-like food
Cup	Bilbo took this item, which made Smaug angry
Dain	Leader of the dwarves after Thorin died
Dale	Town ruins in the shadow of the mountain
Durin's	___ Elf New Year; ___ Day
Dwarf	Dwalin, Bifur, or Dori, for example
Eagles	Saved Thorin & Co. from the wargs & goblins
Elrond	King of the Elves
Elves	Dwarves thought these creatures were foolish
Esgaroth	Lake town
Five	Battle of ___ Armies
Gandalf	___ Wizard
Glamdring	The Foe Hammer
Goblin	Azog, for example
Gollum	___ Pale-eyed water creature
Green	The _____ Dragon Inn
Hobbit	Bilbo, for example
Homely	Last _____ Home; Elrond's home
Key	It opened the secret door in the mountain
King	Elrond was ___ of the Elves
Lights	The Travelers left the path to see what was at these
Lone	_____ Lands; where Bilbo first wished he were back home
Lonely	_____ Mountain; where Smaug lived
Map	Gandalf gave Thorin this and a key
Mirkwood	Never leave the path in this place
Misty	_____ Mountains
Mountain	Misty or Lonely
Necklace	Bilbo's gift to Elvenking to repay his hospitality
Necromancer	Council of Wizards drove the ___ out of southern Mirkwood
Orcrist	The Goblin Cleaver

Unit Word List Continued

Path	Never leave the ____ in Mirkwood
Pinecones	Gandalf lit them on fire and threw them at the wargs
Pipe	Bilbo's smoking device
Pockets	Gollum couldn't guess what was in Bilbo's ____
Ponies	Beorn loaned these as transportation for the travelers
Ravenhill	Old watch post on SW side of mountain
Riddles	Bilbo and Gollum's game
Ring	Gollum's birthday present that Bilbo found
Rivendell	Land of the elves
Roäc	Raven; son of Carc
Secret	Travelers looked for the ___ entrance to the mountain
Shadow	Bilbo's showed even when he wore the ring
Smaug	Dragon
Smell	Smaug's sense of ___ was keen
Smoke	Smaug's puff
Spiders	Killing one gave Bilbo confidence
Sting	Bilbo's name for his knife
Stone	Trolls turned to ___ in the sunlight
Swords	Gandalf and Thorin took ___ from the trolls' cave
Thorin	His grandfather was King of the Mountain
Thrushes	Tame messenger birds
Tolkien	Author
Took	The ___ in Bilbo made him adventurous
Treasure	Smaug slept on it
Trees	Thorin & Co. climbed in them to avoid wargs
Troll	Bert, Tom, or William for example
Wargs	Evil wolves
William	Troll who caught Bilbo trying to pick his pocket
Woodelves	Captured the dwarves and actually saved them

VOCABULARY RESOURCE MATERIALS

VOCABULARY WORD SEARCH - The Hobbit

```
L M C W R Y T C Q U M A W L G W B Z K G
Q D R O U G H T T U N I C U H I N D E R
G U W H N F Y O S T I C F R K O E W A O
N E A I E X H T I B A Z A E I D A N E T
L T N Y S N E Q L S V V I N N K S R D A
P A P N D R U D O M T R G E N O O B D R
W I L Z I I C S A P Y P M P M Y R U Y I
S R I N T H G R T E U A W G L M C S I P
U U G Y A V A Q H R Q L I G L D E T N S
S F H R N U R S S P U A L B E P R L G N
P N T Y D E I U O E E R Y Z D E O E A O
I I K I F R I X M T S D I P I R U L B C
C J N E E N D N E U T E W I N I S B S Y
I G R P G P A M O A S R R N E L K A U S
O P O R P I L I C L F S O N V O F R R V
N S P M D Z B U W L D C U A I U G T D M
E T H R E U M Y N Y B E G C T S C E B W
M T A N D M T V S D S Y H L A S R N V Z
A U D A C I O U S I E Z T E B O T E Y V
G W K H M C Q I C X S R X Z L X G P W N
D J Q N C X S E R X T N F P E G F M G M
B F E P J C R Y W S G J M F H Q R I Y B
K B N K F P P W S N O I T A D E R P E D
```

ABSURD	GUARDIAN	MARAUDING	QUEST
AMENDED	HART	MEMOIRS	RANSOM
ANTIQUITY	HINDER	MUSTERING	REPOSE
AUDACIOUS	HOARD	PERILOUS	RUNES
BUSTLE	HOIST	PERISH	SEIZED
CONSPIRATOR	IMPENETRABLE	PERPETUALLY	SORCEROUS
DELL	IMPLORE	PINNACLE	SUSPICION
DEPREDATIONS	INEVITABLE	PLIGHT	TUNIC
DROUGHT	INFURIATE	PLUNDER	UNCANNY
DUBIOUS	KIN	PRECISE	VAIN
EDDYING	LARDERS	PREFER	WANING
ENMITY	LOATHSOME	PURSUING	WILY
EYRIE	LURE	QUAY	WROUGHT

VOCABULARY WORD SEARCH ANSWER KEY - The Hobbit

ABSURD	GUARDIAN	MARAUDING	QUEST
AMENDED	HART	MEMOIRS	RANSOM
ANTIQUITY	HINDER	MUSTERING	REPOSE
AUDACIOUS	HOARD	PERILOUS	RUNES
BUSTLE	HOIST	PERISH	SEIZED
CONSPIRATOR	IMPENETRABLE	PERPETUALLY	SORCEROUS
DELL	IMPLORE	PINNACLE	SUSPICION
DEPREDATIONS	INEVITABLE	PLIGHT	TUNIC
DROUGHT	INFURIATE	PLUNDER	UNCANNY
DUBIOUS	KIN	PRECISE	VAIN
EDDYING	LARDERS	PREFER	WANING
ENMITY	LOATHSOME	PURSUING	WILY
EYRIE	LURE	QUAY	WROUGHT

VOCABULARY CROSSWORD *The Hobbit*

VOCABULARY CROSSWORD CLUES *The Hobbit*

Across
1. Ask or beg urgently
5. Grabbed
6. Daring; bold
9. Relatives
10. Small, secluded, wooded valley
12. Rest
13. Male deer
15. Nest built on a high place
16. Wharf or reinforced bank where ships are loaded
18. Long, loose-fitting shirt or coat
20. Narrative of experiences an author has lived through
22. Exact
24. Long period of time with no rain
26. Stolen property
29. Entice; attract
32. Release, give up, or free in return for payment
33. Doubtful
34. Lacking substance; hollow; fruitless
35. Ro like better; rather
36. Chasing

Down
1. To make angry; enrage
2. Situation of difficulty
3. Going against the current, esp. in a swirling motion
4. Lift up
5. Thinking something exists, esp. something wrong, without any proof
6. Quality of being very old or ancient
7. One who joins in planning or plotting
8. In command of magic, spells and witchcraft
10. Acts of preying upon others
11. Repulsive; disgusting
14. Words written in ancient Germanic letters
16. Search
17. Delay; get in the way of
19. Unexplainable & strange, exciting wonder and fear
21. Required; necessary
23. A gathered, hidden or stolen supply or treasure
25. One who guards, protects or defends
27. Pantry or cupboards containing food stores
28. Die; pass from existence
30. Deep hatred
31. Commotion; hurried activity

VOCABULARY CROSSWORD ANSWER KEY *The Hobbit*

VOCABULARY MATCHING 1 - The Hobbit

___ 1. ABOMINABLE   A. Going against the main current, especially in a swirling motion

___ 2. GUARDIAN   B. Release, give up or free in return for payment

___ 3. DROUGHT   C. Stolen property

___ 4. REMUNERATION   D. Narrative of experiences an author has lived through

___ 5. IMPLORE   E. Long period of time with no rain

___ 6. LOATHSOME   F. Delay; get in the way of

___ 7. PERILOUS   G. Ask or beg urgently

___ 8. AUDACIOUS   H. Repulsive; disgusting

___ 9. PINNACLE   I. Exact

___ 10. MUSTERING   J. Payment

___ 11. HINDER   K. Gathering

___ 12. MEMOIRS   L. Journey undertaken with a definite objective

___ 13. PREFER   M. Pantry or cupboards containing food stores

___ 14. LARDERS   N. Ridiculous

___ 15. PLUNDER   O. Wharf of reinforced bank where ships are loaded

___ 16. HOARD   P. Surprised

___ 17. ABSURD   Q. One who guards, protects or defends

___ 18. ASTONISHED   R. Wandering in search of something to steal

___ 19. RANSOM   S. Situation of difficulty

___ 20. EDDYING   T. To like better; rather

___ 21. EXPEDITION   U. Thoroughly unpleasant

___ 22. PRECISE   V. Dangerous

___ 23. MARAUDING   W. A gathered, hidden, or stored supply or treasure

___ 24. PLIGHT   X. Daring; bold

___ 25. QUAY   Y. Top; high point

VOCABULARY MATCHING ANSWER KEY 1 - The Hobbit

U - 1. ABOMINABLE	A.	Going against the main current, especially in a swirling motion
Q - 2. GUARDIAN	B.	Release, give up or free in return for payment
E - 3. DROUGHT	C.	Stolen property
J - 4. REMUNERATION	D.	Narrative of experiences an author has lived through
G - 5. IMPLORE	E.	Long period of time with no rain
H - 6. LOATHSOME	F.	Delay; get in the way of
V - 7. PERILOUS	G.	Ask or beg urgently
X - 8. AUDACIOUS	H.	Repulsive; disgusting
Y - 9. PINNACLE	I.	Exact
K - 10. MUSTERING	J.	Payment
F - 11. HINDER	K.	Gathering
D - 12. MEMOIRS	L.	Journey undertaken with a definite objective
T - 13. PREFER	M.	Pantry or cupboards containing food stores
M - 14. LARDERS	N.	Ridiculous
C - 15. PLUNDER	O.	Wharf of reinforced bank where ships are loaded
W - 16. HOARD	P.	Surprised
N - 17. ABSURD	Q.	One who guards, protects or defends
P - 18. ASTONISHED	R.	Wandering in search of something to steal
B - 19. RANSOM	S.	Situation of difficulty
A - 20. EDDYING	T.	To like better; rather
L - 21. EXPEDITION	U.	Thoroughly unpleasant
I - 22. PRECISE	V.	Dangerous
R - 23. MARAUDING	W.	A gathered, hidden, or stored supply or treasure
S - 24. PLIGHT	X.	Daring; bold
O - 25. QUAY	Y.	Top; high point

VOCABULARY MATCHING 2 - The Hobbit

___ 1. TUNIC   A. Ridiculous
___ 2. HOARD   B. Grabbed
___ 3. SUSPICION   C. Nest built on a high place
___ 4. GUARDIAN   D. Doubtful
___ 5. UNIMPEACHABLE E. To like better; rather
___ 6. PLIGHT   F. A gathered, hidden, or stored supply or treasure
___ 7. DEPREDATIONS   G. Acts of preying upon others
___ 8. EDDYING   H. Wharf of reinforced bank where ships are loaded
___ 9. EYRIE   I. Rest
___10. KIN   J. Beyond all doubt; unquestionable
___11. RUNES   K. Top; high point
___12. ABSURD   L. Words written in ancient Germanic letters
___13. PREFER   M. Pantry or cupboards containing food stores
___14. LARDERS   N. Chasing
___15. SEIZED   O. Relatives
___16. UNCANNY   P. Quality of being very old or ancient
___17. PINNACLE   Q. Repulsive; disgusting
___18. BUSTLE   R. Wandering in search of something to steal
___19. REPOSE   S. Long, loose-fitting shirt or coat
___20. LOATHSOME   T. Unexplainable and strange, exciting wonder and fear
___21. PURSUING   U. Situation of difficulty
___22. QUAY   V. Thinking something exists, especially something wrong, without any proof
___23. DUBIOUS   W. One who guards, protects or defends
___24. ANTIQUITY   X. Going against the main current, especially in a swirling motion
___25. MARAUDING   Y. Commotion; hurried activity

VOCABULARY MATCHING ANSWER KEY 2 - The Hobbit

S - 1.	TUNIC	A.	Ridiculous
F - 2.	HOARD	B.	Grabbed
V - 3.	SUSPICION	C.	Nest built on a high place
W - 4.	GUARDIAN	D.	Doubtful
J - 5.	UNIMPEACHABLE	E.	To like better; rather
U - 6.	PLIGHT	F.	A gathered, hidden, or stored supply or treasure
G - 7.	DEPREDATIONS	G.	Acts of preying upon others
X - 8.	EDDYING	H.	Wharf of reinforced bank where ships are loaded
C - 9.	EYRIE	I.	Rest
O - 10.	KIN	J.	Beyond all doubt; unquestionable
L - 11.	RUNES	K.	Top; high point
A - 12.	ABSURD	L.	Words written in ancient Germanic letters
E - 13.	PREFER	M.	Pantry or cupboards containing food stores
M - 14.	LARDERS	N.	Chasing
B - 15.	SEIZED	O.	Relatives
T - 16.	UNCANNY	P.	Quality of being very old or ancient
K - 17.	PINNACLE	Q.	Repulsive; disgusting
Y - 18.	BUSTLE	R.	Wandering in search of something to steal
I - 19.	REPOSE	S.	Long, loose-fitting shirt or coat
Q - 20.	LOATHSOME	T.	Unexplainable and strange, exciting wonder and fear
N - 21.	PURSUING	U.	Situation of difficulty
H - 22.	QUAY	V.	Thinking something exists, especially something wrong, without any proof
D - 23.	DUBIOUS	W.	One who guards, protects or defends
P - 24.	ANTIQUITY	X.	Going against the main current, especially in a swirling motion
R - 25.	MARAUDING	Y.	Commotion; hurried activity

VOCABULARY JUGGLE LETTER 1 - The Hobbit
JUGGLE WITH CLUES

1. EEITBIAVLN   = 1. _____
                         Unavoidable

2. GUNTMERSI   = 2. _____
                         Gathering

3. RIEUSLOP   = 3. _____
                         Dangerous

4. QTEUS   = 4. _____
                         Search

5. DORTGUH   = 5. _____
                         Long period of time with no rain

6. LBNBEOAIAM   = 6. _____
                         Thoroughly unpleasant

7. EIEYR   = 7. _____
                         Nest built on a high place

8. IAUITQYTN   = 8. _____
                         Quality of being very old or ancient

9. DPERNLU   = 9. _____
                         Stolen property

10. ARIDANGU   =10. _____
                         One who guards, protects or defends

11. RTHA   =11. _____
                         Male deer

12. NIK   =12. _____
                         Relatives

13. MPRILOE   =13. _____
                         Ask or beg urgently

14. RSPICEE   =14. _____
                         Exact

15. CTINU   =15. _____
                         Long, loose-fitting shirt or coat

16. DIZEES   =16. _____
                            Grabbed

17. TIRAUFNIE   =17. _____
                            To make angry; enrage

18. TOCNRPSAOIR   =18. _____
                            One who joins in planning or plotting

19. EBTNPMERIAEL   =19. _____
                            Cant's be pierced or entered through

20. TIPLHG   =20. _____
                            Situation of difficulty

21. EERFPR   =21. _____
                            To like better; rather

22. ELRU   =22. _____
                            Entice; attract

23. OMNSAR   =23. _____
                            Release, give up or free in return for payment

24. CNPILNEA   =24. _____
                            Top; high point

25. TPEEIDNOXI   =25. _____
                            Journey undertaken with a definite objective

26. LELD   =26. _____
                            Small, secluded, wooded valley

27. NIYMTE   =27. _____
                            Deep hatred

28. TSOIH   =28. _____
                            Lift up

29. SHIRPE   =29. _____
                            Die; pass from existence

VOCABULARY JUGGLE LETTER ANSWER KEY 1 - The Hobbit

1. EEITBIAVLN = 1. INEVITABLE
   Unavoidable

2. GUNTMERSI = 2. MUSTERING
   Gathering

3. RIEUSLOP = 3. PERILOUS
   Dangerous

4. QTEUS = 4. QUEST
   Search

5. DORTGUH = 5. DROUGHT
   Long period of time with no rain

6. LBNBEOAIAM = 6. ABOMINABLE
   Thoroughly unpleasant

7. EIEYR = 7. EYRIE
   Nest built on a high place

8. IAUITQYTN = 8. ANTIQUITY
   Quality of being very old or ancient

9. DPERNLU = 9. PLUNDER
   Stolen property

10. ARIDANGU =10. GUARDIAN
    One who guards, protects or defends

11. RTHA =11. HART
    Male deer

12. NIK =12. KIN
    Relatives

13. MPRILOE =13. IMPLORE
    Ask or beg urgently

14. RSPICEE =14. PRECISE
    Exact

15. CTINU =15. TUNIC
    Long, loose-fitting shirt or coat

16. DIZEES =16. SEIZED
Grabbed

17. TIRAUFNIE =17. INFURIATE
To make angry; enrage

18. TOCNRPSAOIR =18. CONSPIRATOR
One who joins in planning or plotting

19. EBTNPMERIAEL =19. IMPENETRABLE
Cant's be pierced or entered through

20. TIPLHG =20. PLIGHT
Situation of difficulty

21. EERFPR =21. PREFER
To like better; rather

22. ELRU =22. LURE
Entice; attract

23. OMNSAR =23. RANSOM
Release, give up or free in return for payment

24. CNPILNEA =24. PINNACLE
Top; high point

25. TPEEIDNOXI =25. EXPEDITION
Journey undertaken with a definite objective

26. LELD =26. DELL
Small, secluded, wooded valley

27. NIYMTE =27. ENMITY
Deep hatred

28. TSOIH =28. HOIST
Lift up

29. SHIRPE =29. PERISH
Die; pass from existence

VOCABULARY JUGGLE LETTER 2 - The Hobbit

1. OBUDISU = 1. _____
   Doubtful

2. USINSCIPO = 2. _____
   Thinking something exists, especially something wrong, without any proof

3. CUNNANY = 3. _____
   Unexplainable and strange, exciting wonder and fear

4. RWUTHGO = 4. _____
   Shaped; worked

5. RMAIAGUDN = 5. _____
   Wandering in search of something to steal

6. ERUSN = 6. _____
   Words written in ancient Germanic letters

7. RDAHO = 7. _____
   A gathered, hidden, or stored supply or treasure

8. SEIMORM = 8. _____
   Narrative of experiences an author has lived through

9. OOURCSESR = 9. _____
   In command of magic, spells and witchcraft

10. SLREDAR =10. _____
    Pantry or cupboards containing food stores

11. OAAUSICDU =11. _____
    Daring; bold

12. BUADRS =12. _____
    Ridiculous

13. DHNOIETASS =13. _____
    Surprised

14. ENRHID =14. _____
    Delay; get in the way of

15. NOEINTMRRAUE =15. _____
    Payment

16. IQERUISTE =16. _____
Required, necessary

17. EOERSP =17. _____
Rest

18. UPNGSIUR =18. _____
Chasing

19. UYAQ =19. _____
Wharf of reinforced bank where ships are loaded

20. LRPEPAULETY =20. _____
Continuously; always

21. IVAN =21. _____
Lacking substance; hollow; fruitless

22. ELUBST =22. _____
Commotion; hurried activity

23. GDDIENY =23. _____
Going against the main current, especially in a swirling motion

24. EBAMPLUIENCHA =24. _____
Beyond all doubt; unquestionable

25. DADEMEN =25. _____
Corrected; made better

26. NGNIWA =26. _____
Lessening; going away; ending

27. SAEDPEOIRNDT =27. _____
Acts of preying upon others

28. IWLY =28. _____
Calculating; plotting

29. OTMHELASO =29. _____
Repulsive; disgusting

VOCABULARY JUGGLE LETTER ANSWER KEY 2 - The Hobbit

1. OBUDISU = 1. DUBIOUS
   Doubtful

2. USINSCIPO = 2. SUSPICION
   Thinking something exists, especially something wrong, without any proof

3. CUNNANY = 3. UNCANNY
   Unexplainable and strange, exciting wonder and fear

4. RWUTHGO = 4. WROUGHT
   Shaped; worked

5. RMAIAGUDN = 5. MARAUDING
   Wandering in search of something to steal

6. ERUSN = 6. RUNES
   Words written in ancient Germanic letters

7. RDAHO = 7. HOARD
   A gathered, hidden, or stored supply or treasure

8. SEIMORM = 8. MEMOIRS
   Narrative of experiences an author has lived through

9. OOURCSESR = 9. SORCEROUS
   In command of magic, spells and witchcraft

10. SLREDAR =10. LARDERS
    Pantry or cupboards containing food stores

11. OAAUSICDU =11. AUDACIOUS
    Daring; bold

12. BUADRS =12. ABSURD
    Ridiculous

13. DHNOIETASS =13. ASTONISHED
    Surprised

14. ENRHID =14. HINDER
    Delay; get in the way of

15. NOEINTMRRAUE =15. REMUNERATION
    Payment

16. IQERUISTE =16. REQUISITE
Required, necessary

17. EOERSP =17. REPOSE
Rest

18. UPNGSIUR =18. PURSUING
Chasing

19. UYAQ =19. QUAY
Wharf of reinforced bank where ships are loaded

20. LRPEPAULETY =20. PERPETUALLY
Continuously; always

21. IVAN =21. VAIN
Lacking substance; hollow; fruitless

22. ELUBST =22. BUSTLE
Commotion; hurried activity

23. GDDIENY =23. EDDYING
Going against the main current, especially in a swirling motion

24. EBAMPLUIENCHA =24. UNIMPEACHABLE
Beyond all doubt; unquestionable

25. DADEMEN =25. AMENDED
Corrected; made better

26. NGNIWA =26. WANING
Lessening; going away; ending

27. SAEDPEOIRNDT =27. DEPREDATIONS
Acts of preying upon others

28. IWLY =28. WILY
Calculating; plotting

29. OTMHELASO =29. LOATHSOME
Repulsive; disgusting

VOCABULARY WORD LIST *The Hobbit*

Abominable	Thoroughly unpleasant
Absurd	Ridiculous
Amended	Corrected; made better
Antiquity	Quality of being very old or ancient
Astonished	Surprised
Audacious	Daring; bold
Bustle	Commotion; hurried activity
Conspirator	One who joins in planning or plotting
Dell	Small, secluded, wooded valley
Depredations	Acts of preying upon others
Drought	Long period of time with no rain
Dubious	Doubtful
Eddying	Going against the main current, especially in a swirling motion
Enmity	Deep hatred
Expedition	Journey undertaken with a definite objective
Eyrie	Nest built on a high place
Guardian	One who guards, protects or defends
Hart	Male deer
Hinder	Delay; get in the way of
Hoard	A gathered, hidden, or stored supply or treasure
Hoist	Lift up
Impenetrable	Can't be pierced or entered through
Implore	Ask or beg urgently
Inevitable	Unavoidable
Infuriate	To make angry; enrage
Kin	Relatives
Larders	Pantry or cupboards containing food stores
Loathsome	Repulsive; disgusting
Lure	Entice; attract
Marauding	Wandering in search of something to steal
Memoirs	Narrative of experiences an author has lived through
Mustering	Gathering
Perilous	Dangerous
Perish	Die; pass from existence
Perpetually	Continuously; always
Pinnacle	Top; high point
Plight	Situation of difficulty
Plunder	Stolen property
Precise	Exact
Prefer	To like better; rather
Pursuing	Chasing
Quay	Wharf or reinforced bank where ships are loaded

Hobbit Vocabulary Word List Continued:

Quest	Search
Ransom	Release, give up or free in return for payment
Remuneration	Payment
Repose	Rest
Requisite	Required, necessary
Runes	Words written in ancient Germanic letters
Seized	Grabbed
Sorcerous	In command of magic, spells and witchcraft
Suspicion	Thinking something exists, especially something wrong, without any proof
Tunic	Long, loose-fitting shirt or coat
Uncanny	Unexplainable and strange, exciting wonder and fear
Unimpeachable	Beyond all doubt; unquestionable
Vain	Lacking substance; hollow; fruitless
Waning	Lessening; going away; ending
Wily	Calculating; plotting
Wrought	Shaped; worked

www.ingramcontent.com/pod-product-compliance
Lightning Source LLC
Chambersburg PA
CBHW051405070526
44584CB00023B/3304